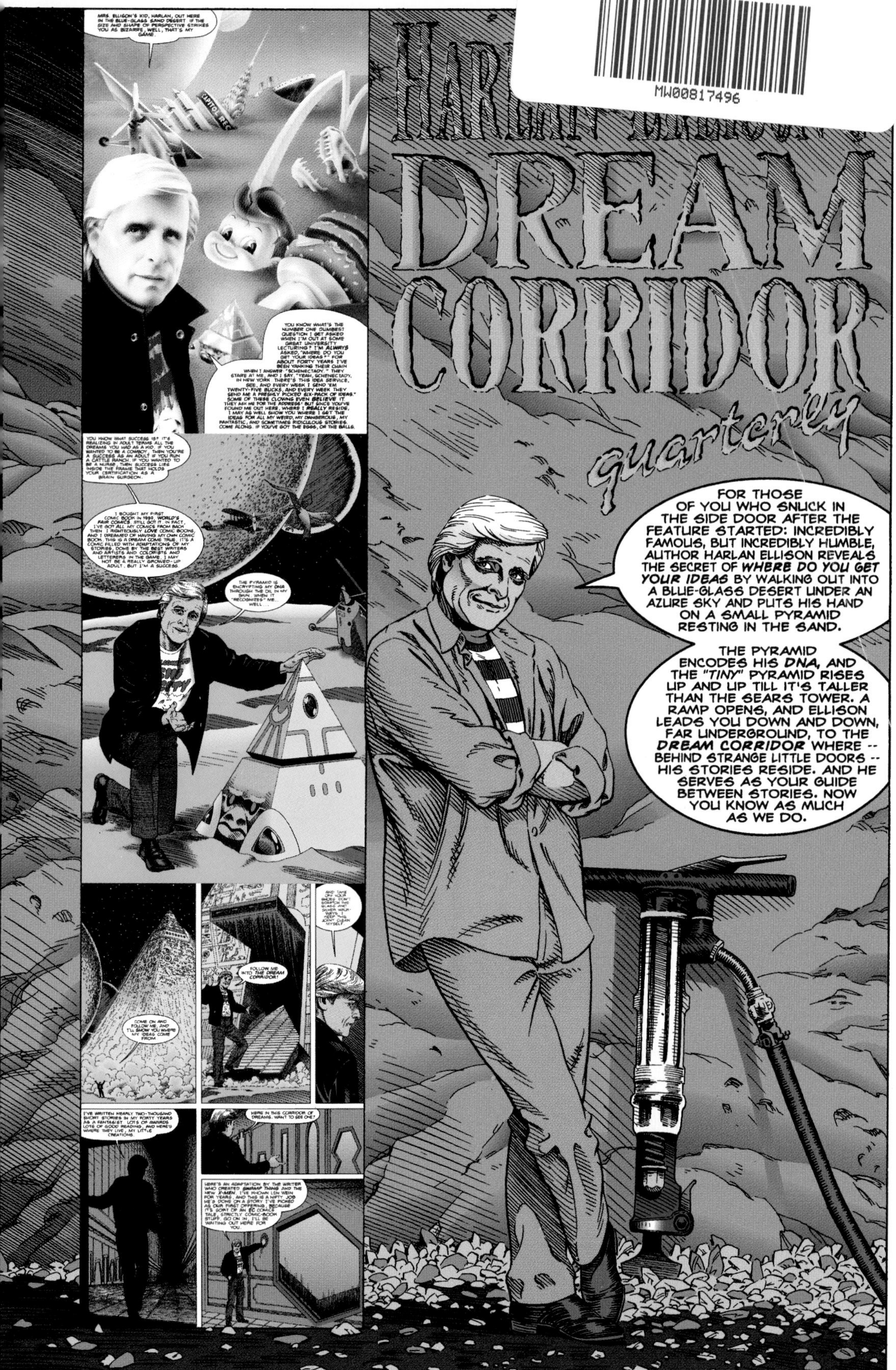
DREAM
CORRIDOR
quarterly
MRS. ELLISON'S KID, HARLAN, OUT HERE IN THE BLUE-GLASS SAND DESERT. IF THE SIZE AND SHAPE OF PERSPECTIVE STRIKES YOU AS BIZARRE, WELL, THAT'S MY GAME.
YOU KNOW WHAT'S THE NUMBER ONE DUMBEST QUESTION I GET ASKED WHEN I'M OUT AT SOME GREAT UNIVERSITY LECTURING? I'M ALWAYS ASKED, "WHERE DO YOU GET YOUR IDEAS?" FOR ABOUT FORTY YEARS I'VE BEEN YANKING THEIR CHAIN WHEN I ANSWER: "SCHENECTADY." THEY STARE AT ME, AND I SAY, "YEAH, SCHENECTADY, IN NEW YORK. THERE'S THIS IDEA SERVICE, SEE, AND EVERY WEEK I SEND 'EM TWENTY-FIVE BUCKS, AND EVERY WEEK THEY SEND ME A FRESHLY PICKED SIX-PACK OF IDEAS." SOME OF THESE CLOWNS EVEN BELIEVE IT. THEY ASK ME FOR THE ADDRESS! BUT SINCE YOU'VE FOUND ME OUT HERE, WHERE I REALLY RESIDE, I MAY AS WELL SHOW YOU WHERE I GET THE IDEAS FOR ALL MY WEIRD, MY DANGEROUS, MY FANTASTIC, AND SOMETIMES RIDICULOUS STORIES. COME ALONG. IF YOU'VE GOT THE EGGS, OR THE BALLS.
YOU KNOW WHAT SUCCESS IS? IT'S REALIZING IN ADULT TERMS ALL THE DREAMS YOU HAD AS A KID. IF YOU WANTED TO BE A COWBOY, THEN YOU'RE A SUCCESS AS AN ADULT IF YOU RUN A CATTLE RANCH. IF YOU WANTED TO BE A NURSE, THEN SUCCESS LIES INSIDE THE FRAME THAT HOLDS YOUR CERTIFICATION AS A BRAIN SURGEON.
I BOUGHT MY FIRST COMIC BOOK IN 1939, WORLD'S FAIR COMICS. STILL GOT IT. IN FACT, I'VE GOT ALL MY COMICS FROM BACK THEN. I RIGHTEOUSLY LOVE COMIC BOOKS, AND I DREAMED OF HAVING MY OWN COMIC BOOK. THIS IS A DREAM COME TRUE. IT'S A COMIC FILLED WITH ADAPTATIONS OF MY STORIES, DONE BY THE BEST WRITERS AND ARTISTS AND COLORISTS AND LETTERERS IN THE GAME. I MAY NOT BE A REALLY GROWED-UP ADULT, BUT I'M A SUCCESS.
THE PYRAMID IS ENCRYPTING MY DNA THROUGH THE OIL IN MY SKIN. WHEN IT "RECOGNIZES" ME... WELL...
COME ON AND FOLLOW ME, AND I'LL SHOW YOU WHERE MY IDEAS COME FROM.
FOLLOW ME INTO THE DREAM CORRIDOR!
I'VE WRITTEN NEARLY TWO-THOUSAND SHORT STORIES IN MY FORTY YEARS AS A FANTASIST. LOTS OF AWARDS, LOTS OF GOOD READING, AND HERE'S WHERE THEY LIVE, MY LITTLE CREATIONS.
HERE IN THIS CORRIDOR OF DREAMS. WANT TO SEE ONE?
HERE'S AN ADAPTATION BY THE WRITER WHO CREATED SWAMP THING AND THE NEW X-MEN. I'VE KNOWN LEN WEIN FOR YEARS, AND THIS IS A NIFTY JOB HE'S DONE ON A STORY I'VE PICKED AS OUR FIRST OFFERING, BECAUSE IT'S SORT OF AN EC COMICS TALE, STRICTLY COMIC-BOOK STUFF. GO ON IN. I'LL BE WAITING OUT HERE FOR YOU.
FOR THOSE OF YOU WHO SNUCK IN THE SIDE DOOR AFTER THE FEATURE STARTED: INCREDIBLY FAMOUS, BUT INCREDIBLY HUMBLE, AUTHOR HARLAN ELLISON REVEALS THE SECRET OF WHERE DO YOU GET YOUR IDEAS BY WALKING OUT INTO A BLUE-GLASS DESERT UNDER AN AZURE SKY AND PUTS HIS HAND ON A SMALL PYRAMID RESTING IN THE SAND.
THE PYRAMID ENCODES HIS DNA, AND THE "TINY" PYRAMID RISES UP AND UP TILL IT'S TALLER THAN THE SEARS TOWER. A RAMP OPENS, AND ELLISON LEADS YOU DOWN AND DOWN, FAR UNDERGROUND, TO THE DREAM CORRIDOR WHERE -- BEHIND STRANGE LITTLE DOORS -- HIS STORIES RESIDE. AND HE SERVES AS YOUR GUIDE BETWEEN STORIES. NOW YOU KNOW AS MUCH AS WE DO.

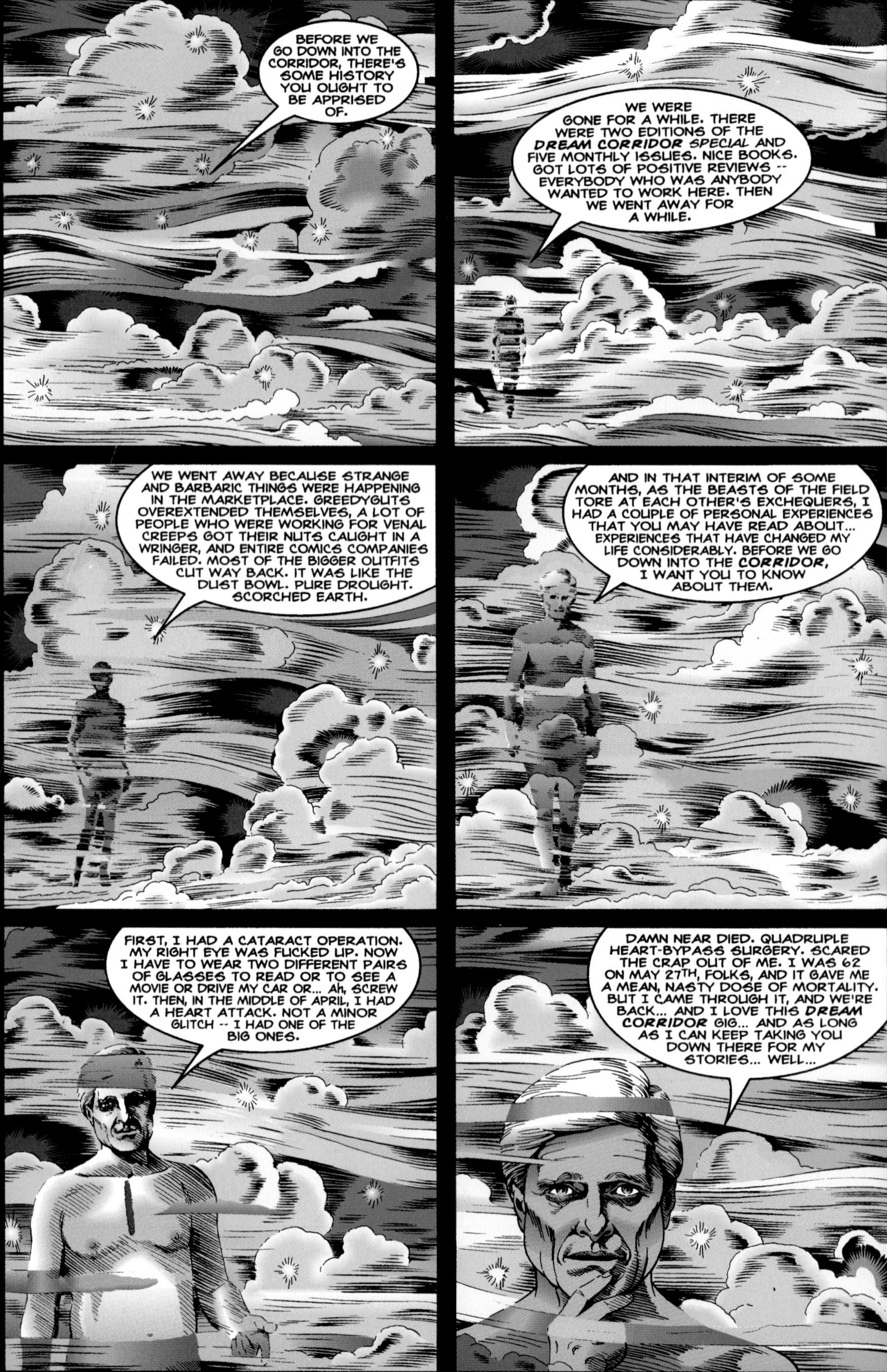
BEFORE WE GO DOWN INTO THE CORRIDOR, THERE'S SOME HISTORY YOU OUGHT TO BE APPRISED OF.
WE WERE GONE FOR A WHILE. THERE WERE TWO EDITIONS OF THE *DREAM CORRIDOR SPECIAL* AND FIVE MONTHLY ISSUES. NICE BOOKS. GOT LOTS OF POSITIVE REVIEWS -- EVERYBODY WHO WAS ANYBODY WANTED TO WORK HERE. THEN WE WENT AWAY FOR A WHILE.
WE WENT AWAY BECAUSE STRANGE AND BARBARIC THINGS WERE HAPPENING IN THE MARKETPLACE. GREEDYGUTS OVEREXTENDED THEMSELVES, A LOT OF PEOPLE WHO WERE WORKING FOR VENAL CREEPS GOT THEIR NUTS CAUGHT IN A WRINGER, AND ENTIRE COMICS COMPANIES FAILED. MOST OF THE BIGGER OUTFITS CUT WAY BACK. IT WAS LIKE THE DUST BOWL. PURE DROUGHT. SCORCHED EARTH.
AND IN THAT INTERIM OF SOME MONTHS, AS THE BEASTS OF THE FIELD TORE AT EACH OTHER'S EXCHEQUERS, I HAD A COUPLE OF PERSONAL EXPERIENCES THAT YOU MAY HAVE READ ABOUT... EXPERIENCES THAT HAVE CHANGED MY LIFE CONSIDERABLY. BEFORE WE GO DOWN INTO THE *CORRIDOR,* I WANT YOU TO KNOW ABOUT THEM.
FIRST, I HAD A CATARACT OPERATION. MY RIGHT EYE WAS FUCKED UP. NOW I HAVE TO WEAR TWO DIFFERENT PAIRS OF GLASSES TO READ OR TO SEE A MOVIE OR DRIVE MY CAR OR... Ah, SCREW IT. THEN, IN THE MIDDLE OF APRIL, I HAD A HEART ATTACK. NOT A MINOR GLITCH -- I HAD ONE OF THE BIG ONES.
DAMN NEAR DIED. QUADRUPLE HEART-BYPASS SURGERY. SCARED THE CRAP OUT OF ME. I WAS 62 ON MAY 27TH, FOLKS, AND IT GAVE ME A MEAN, NASTY DOSE OF MORTALITY. BUT I CAME THROUGH IT, AND WE'RE BACK... AND I LOVE THIS *DREAM CORRIDOR* GIG... AND AS LONG AS I CAN KEEP TAKING YOU DOWN THERE FOR MY STORIES... WELL...

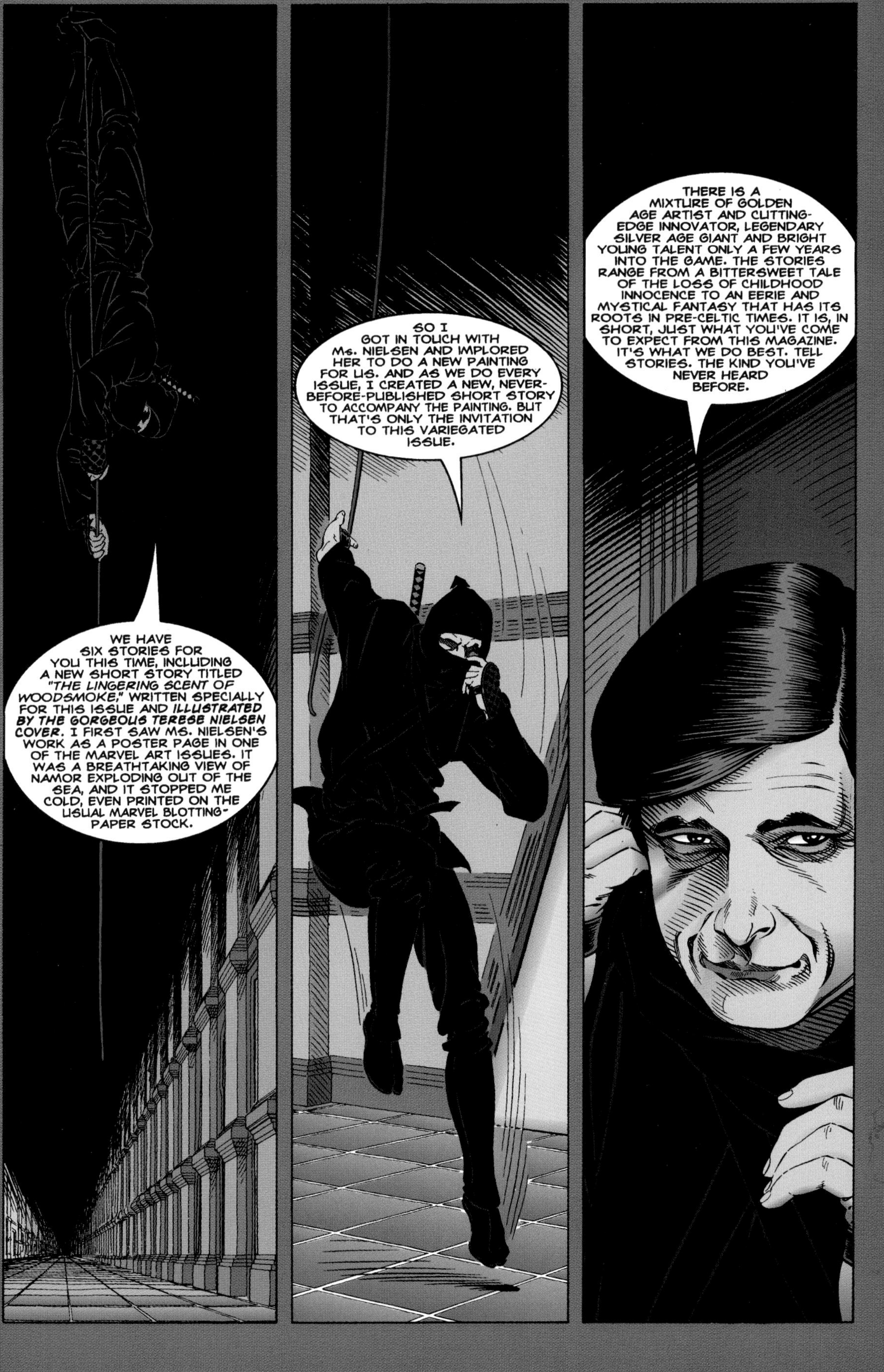

WE HAVE SIX STORIES FOR YOU THIS TIME, INCLUDING A NEW SHORT STORY TITLED "THE LINGERING SCENT OF WOODSMOKE," WRITTEN SPECIALLY FOR THIS ISSUE AND ILLUSTRATED BY THE GORGEOUS TERESE NIELSEN COVER. I FIRST SAW MS. NIELSEN'S WORK AS A POSTER PAGE IN ONE OF THE MARVEL ART ISSUES. IT WAS A BREATHTAKING VIEW OF NAMOR EXPLODING OUT OF THE SEA, AND IT STOPPED ME COLD, EVEN PRINTED ON THE USUAL MARVEL BLOTTING-PAPER STOCK.
SO I GOT IN TOUCH WITH Ms. NIELSEN AND IMPLORED HER TO DO A NEW PAINTING FOR US. AND AS WE DO EVERY ISSUE, I CREATED A NEW, NEVER-BEFORE-PUBLISHED SHORT STORY TO ACCOMPANY THE PAINTING. BUT THAT'S ONLY THE INVITATION TO THIS VARIEGATED ISSUE.
THERE IS A MIXTURE OF GOLDEN AGE ARTIST AND CUTTING-EDGE INNOVATOR, LEGENDARY SILVER AGE GIANT AND BRIGHT YOUNG TALENT ONLY A FEW YEARS INTO THE GAME. THE STORIES RANGE FROM A BITTERSWEET TALE OF THE LOSS OF CHILDHOOD INNOCENCE TO AN EERIE AND MYSTICAL FANTASY THAT HAS ITS ROOTS IN PRE-CELTIC TIMES. IT IS, IN SHORT, JUST WHAT YOU'VE COME TO EXPECT FROM THIS MAGAZINE. IT'S WHAT WE DO BEST. TELL STORIES. THE KIND YOU'VE NEVER HEARD BEFORE.

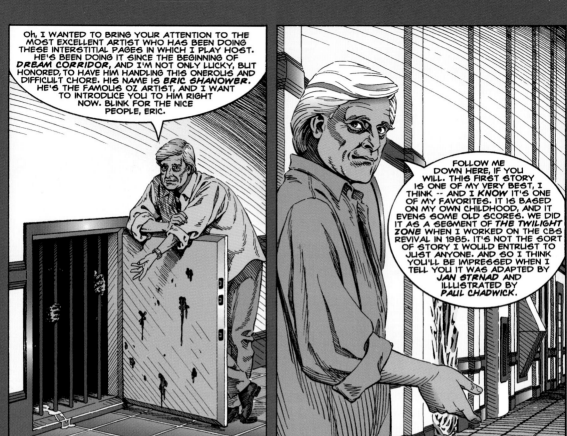

OH, I WANTED TO BRING YOUR ATTENTION TO THE MOST EXCELLENT ARTIST WHO HAS BEEN DOING THESE INTERSTITIAL PAGES IN WHICH I PLAY HOST. HE'S BEEN DOING IT SINCE THE BEGINNING OF *DREAM CORRIDOR*, AND I'M NOT ONLY LUCKY, BUT HONORED, TO HAVE HIM HANDLING THIS ONEROUS AND DIFFICULT CHORE. HIS NAME IS *ERIC SHANOWER*. HE'S THE FAMOUS OZ ARTIST, AND I WANT TO INTRODUCE YOU TO HIM RIGHT NOW. BLINK FOR THE NICE PEOPLE, ERIC.

FOLLOW ME DOWN HERE, IF YOU WILL. THIS FIRST STORY IS ONE OF MY VERY BEST, I THINK -- AND I *KNOW* IT'S ONE OF MY FAVORITES. IT IS BASED ON MY OWN CHILDHOOD, AND IT EVENS SOME OLD SCORES. WE DID IT AS A SEGMENT OF *THE TWILIGHT ZONE* WHEN I WORKED ON THE CBS REVIVAL IN 1985. IT'S NOT THE SORT OF STORY I WOULD ENTRUST TO JUST ANYONE. AND SO I THINK YOU'LL BE IMPRESSED WHEN I TELL YOU IT WAS ADAPTED BY *JAN STRNAD* AND ILLUSTRATED BY *PAUL CHADWICK*.

JAN IS AN OLD FRIEND AND, FOR MY MONEY, ONE OF THE BEST WRITERS IN THIS BUSINESS. I FIRST ENCOUNTERED HIS WORK BACK IN THE 1970s IN THE WARREN MAGAZINES, *CREEPY* AND *EERIE*. THEN, LATER, HE STARTED WORKING WITH RICHARD CORBEN AND THEY DID *MUTANT WORLD*, AND AFTER THAT I WAS ASKED TO DO AN INTRODUCTION TO JAN AND RICHARD'S *NEW TALES OF THE ARABIAN NIGHTS*. JAN REVIVED THE CHARACTER OF THE ATOM FOR DC (AND THEY REWARDED HIM BY GIVING THE REGULAR BOOK TO SOMEONE ELSE), AND FOR THE LAST FEW YEARS HE'S BEEN WORKING IN ANIMATION -- X-MEN, DISNEY -- AND WRITING A HORROR NOVEL TITLED *RETURNS*.

PAUL CHADWICK IS...WELL, WHAT THE HELL IS THERE TO SAY ABOUT PAUL CHADWICK BEYOND THE FACT THAT HE IS THE CREATIVE INTELLECT BEHIND *CONCRETE*, SURELY ONE OF THE BEST HALF-DOZEN CREATIONS TO COME OUT OF THIS VISUAL MEDIUM IN A COUPLE OF DECADES! IN ADDITION, HE IS A MAN OF PRINCIPLE AND A CONSERVATIONIST DEEPLY CONCERNED WITH THE FATE OF THE PLANET. HIS IS A SENSITIVE AND UTTERLY HUMANE NATURE, AND HE BRINGS THAT DELICATE TOUCH TO THIS MOST DIFFICULT OF STORIES TO TRANSLATE INTO ART. I CAN'T THINK OF ANYONE ELSE I WOULD HAVE ENTRUSTED WITH THIS STORY THAT LIES SO CLOSE TO MY HEART AND MEMORY.

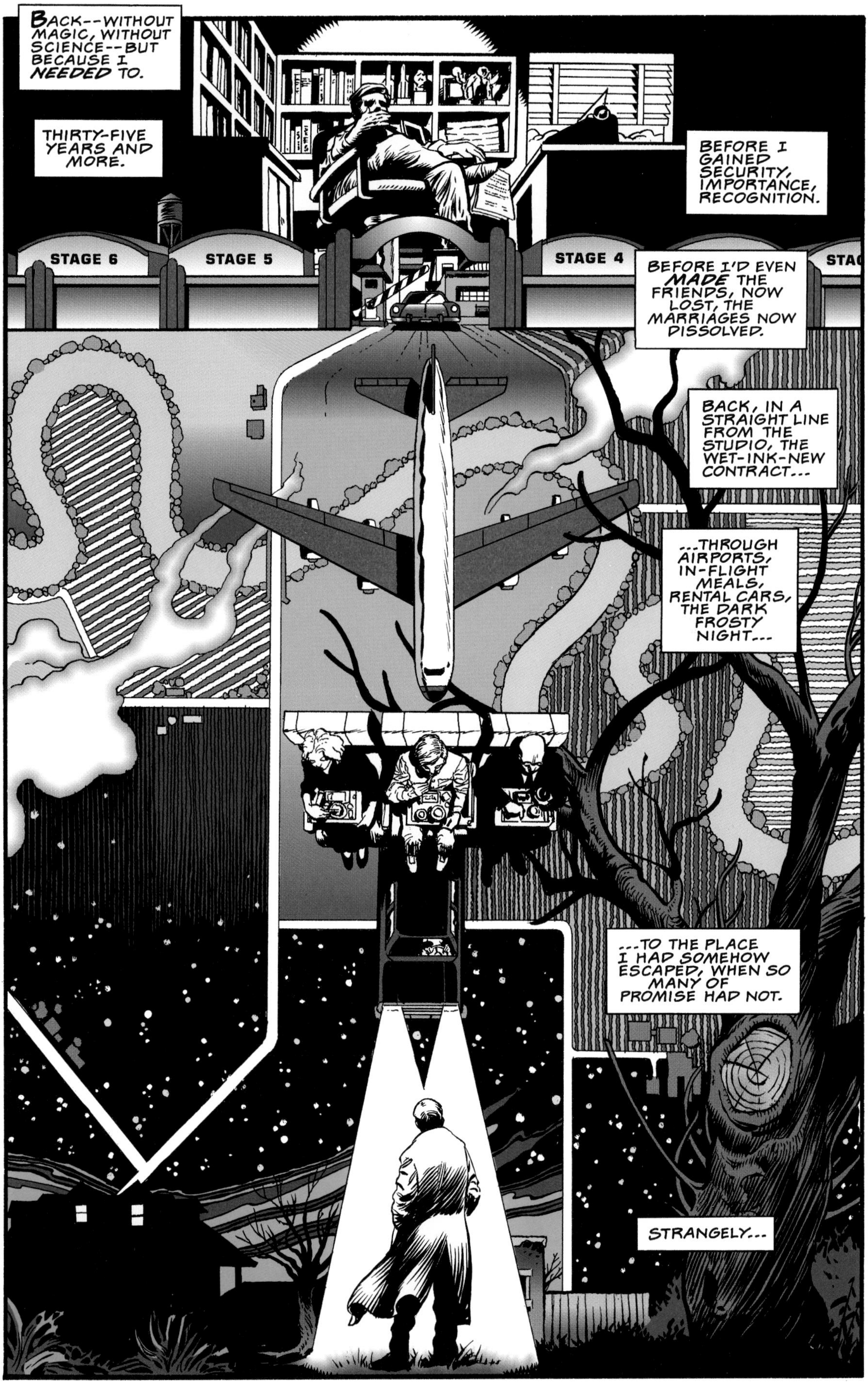
BACK--WITHOUT MAGIC, WITHOUT SCIENCE--BUT BECAUSE I *NEEDED* TO.
THIRTY-FIVE YEARS AND MORE.
BEFORE I GAINED SECURITY, IMPORTANCE, RECOGNITION.
STAGE 6
STAGE 5
STAGE 4
BEFORE I'D EVEN *MADE* THE FRIENDS, NOW LOST, THE MARRIAGES NOW DISSOLVED.
BACK, IN A STRAIGHT LINE FROM THE STUDIO, THE WET-INK-NEW CONTRACT...
...THROUGH AIRPORTS, IN-FLIGHT MEALS, RENTAL CARS, THE DARK FROSTY NIGHT...
...TO THE PLACE I HAD SOMEHOW ESCAPED, WHEN SO MANY OF PROMISE HAD NOT.
STRANGELY...

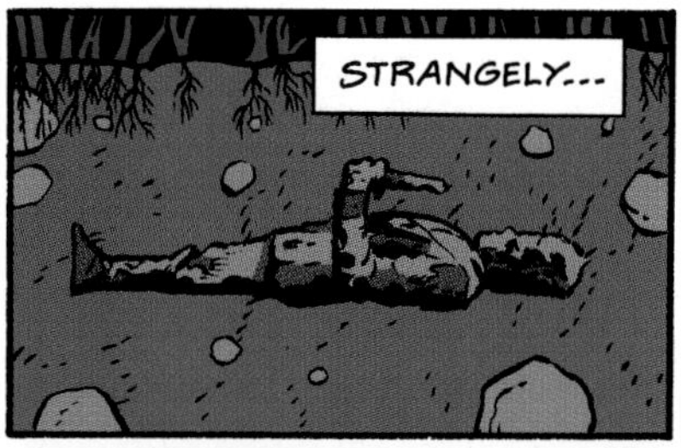
STRANGELY...

ONE LIFE, FURNISHED IN EARLY POVERTY

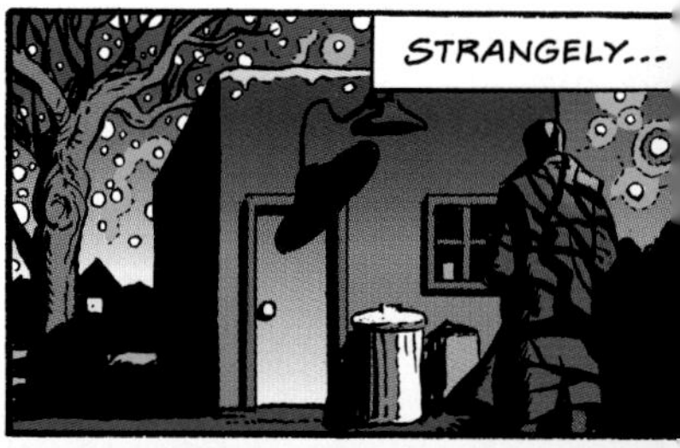
STRANGELY...

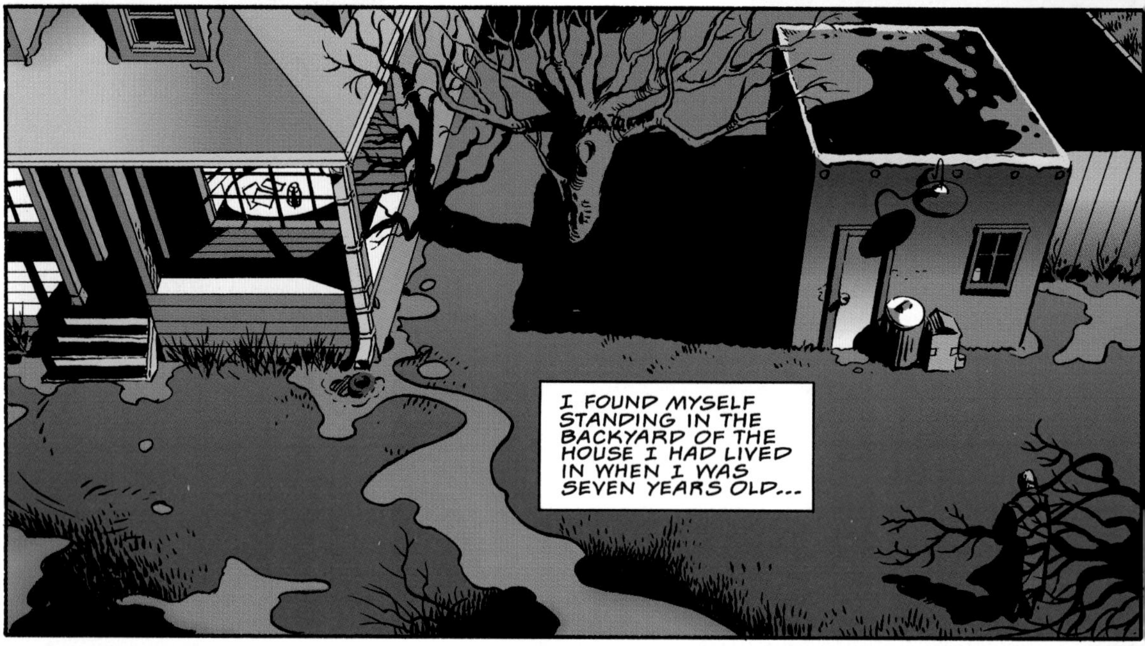
I FOUND MYSELF STANDING IN THE BACKYARD OF THE HOUSE I HAD LIVED IN WHEN I WAS SEVEN YEARS OLD...

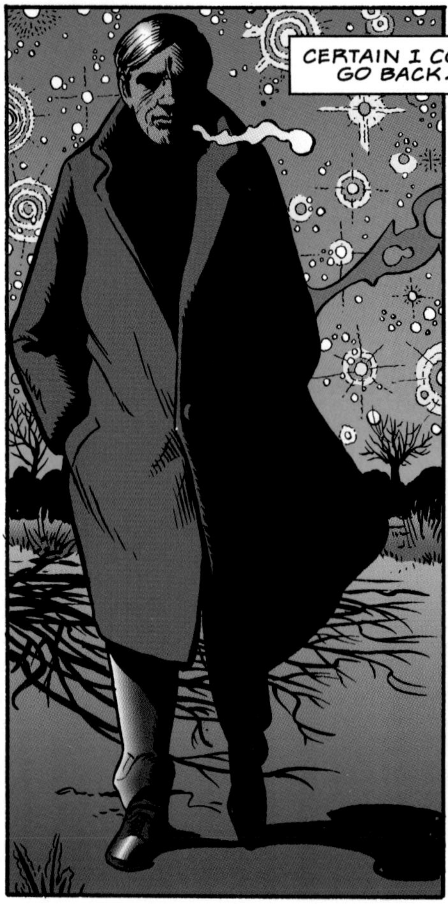
CERTAIN I COULD GO BACK.

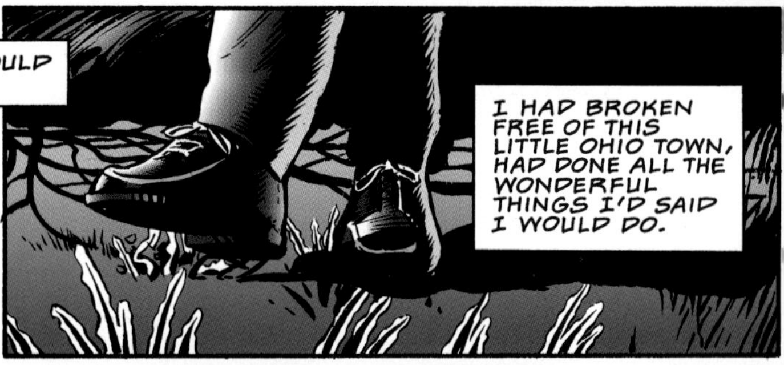
I HAD BROKEN FREE OF THIS LITTLE OHIO TOWN, HAD DONE ALL THE WONDERFUL THINGS I'D SAID I WOULD DO.

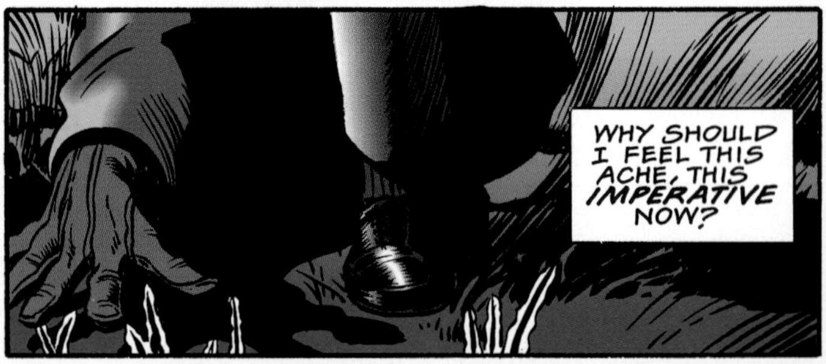
WHY SHOULD I FEEL THIS ACHE, THIS *IMPERATIVE* NOW?

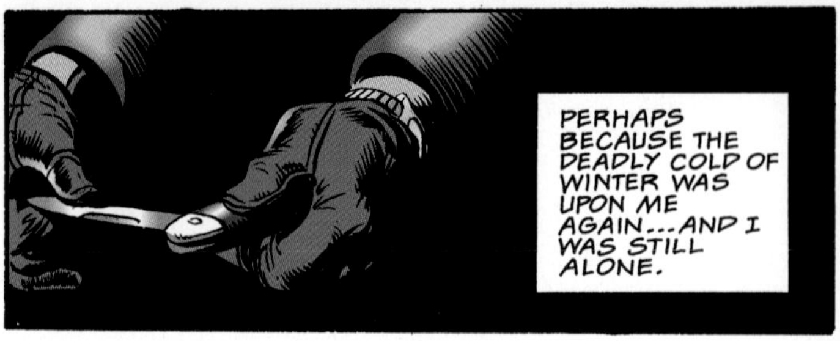
PERHAPS BECAUSE THE DEADLY COLD OF WINTER WAS UPON ME AGAIN... AND I WAS STILL ALONE.

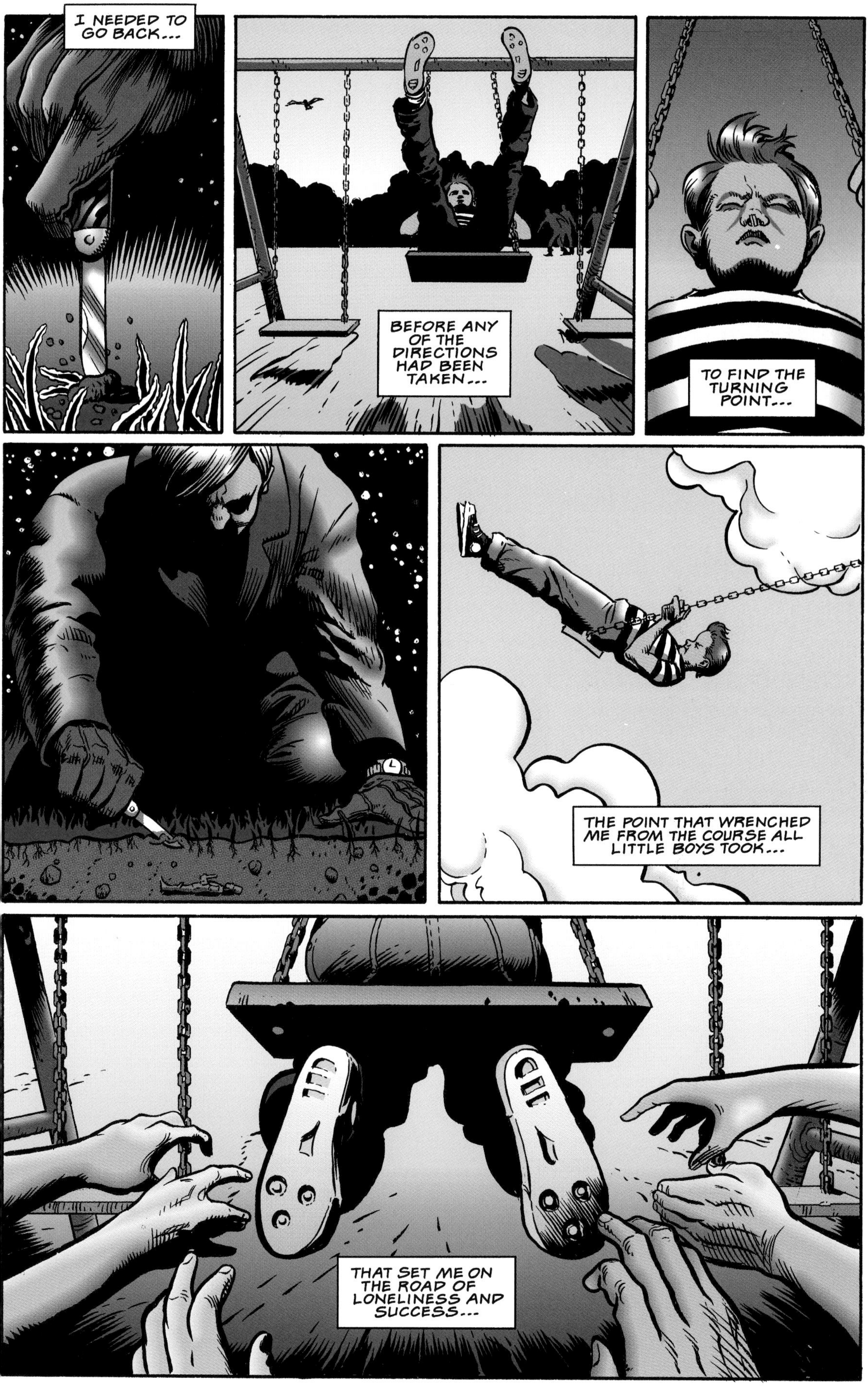
I NEEDED TO GO BACK...
BEFORE ANY OF THE DIRECTIONS HAD BEEN TAKEN...
TO FIND THE TURNING POINT...
THE POINT THAT WRENCHED ME FROM THE COURSE ALL LITTLE BOYS TOOK...
THAT SET ME ON THE ROAD OF LONELINESS AND SUCCESS...

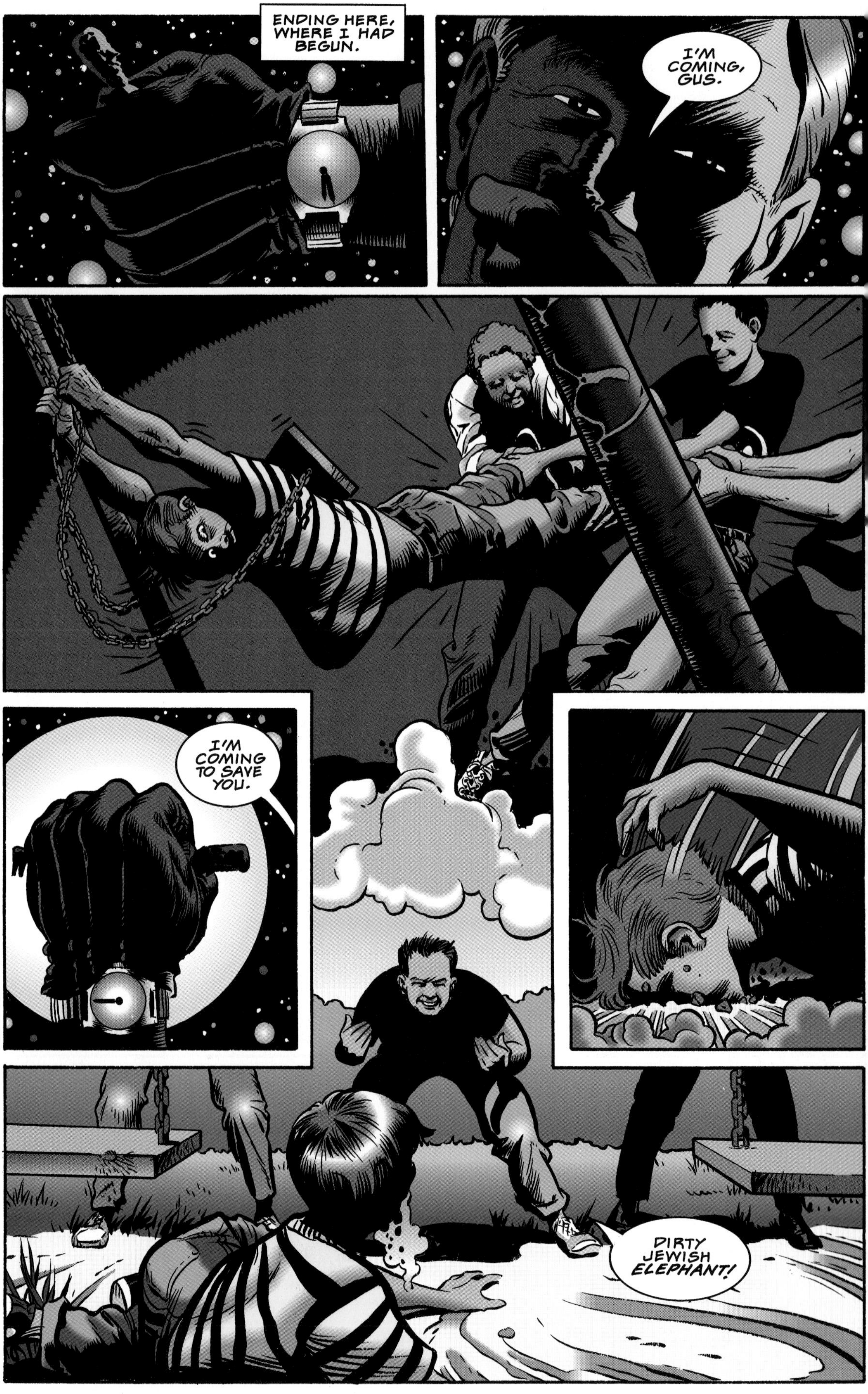
ENDING HERE, WHERE I HAD BEGUN.
I'M COMING, GUS.
I'M COMING TO SAVE YOU.
DIRTY JEWISH ELEPHANT!

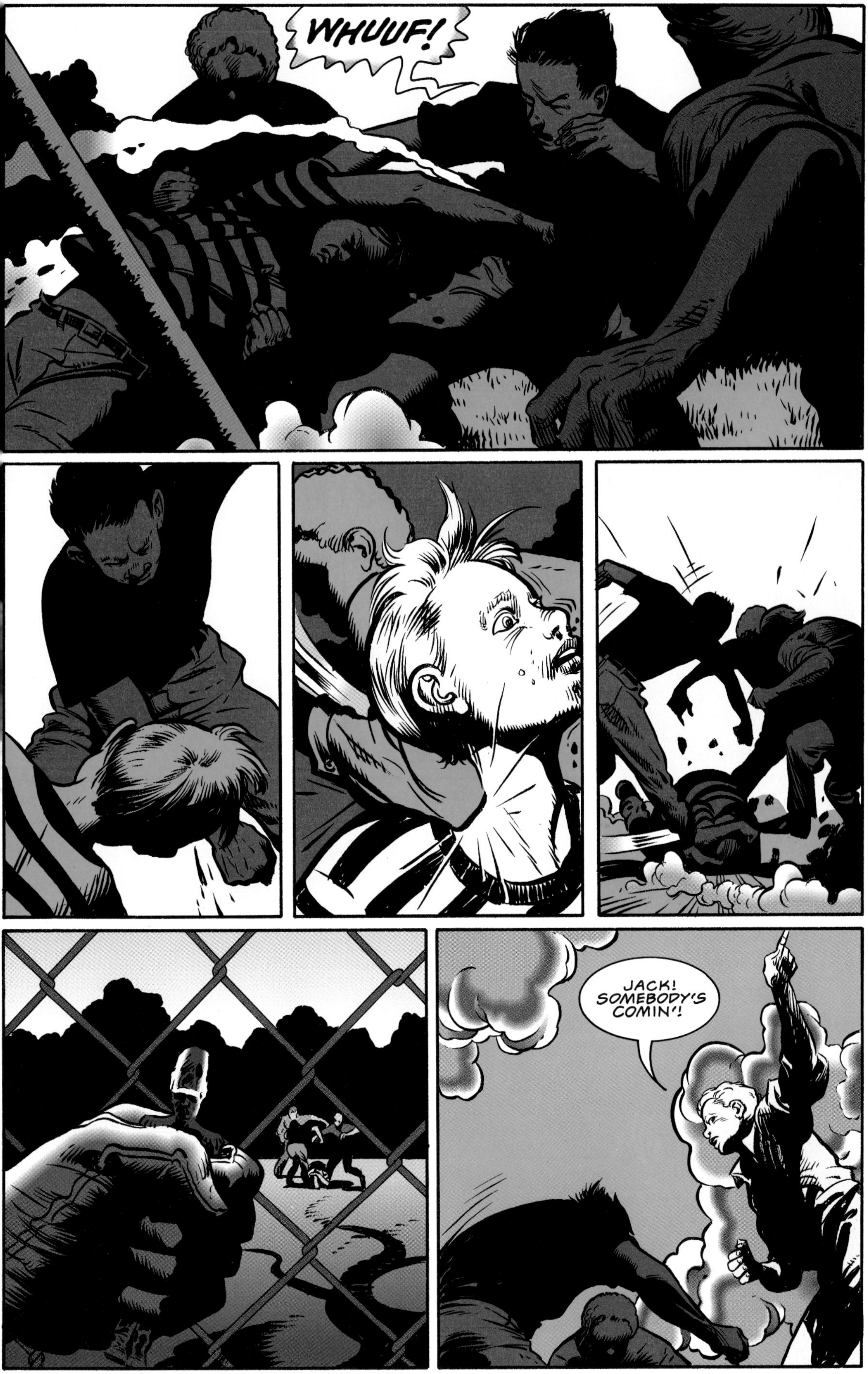
WHUUF!
JACK! SOMEBODY'S COMIN'!

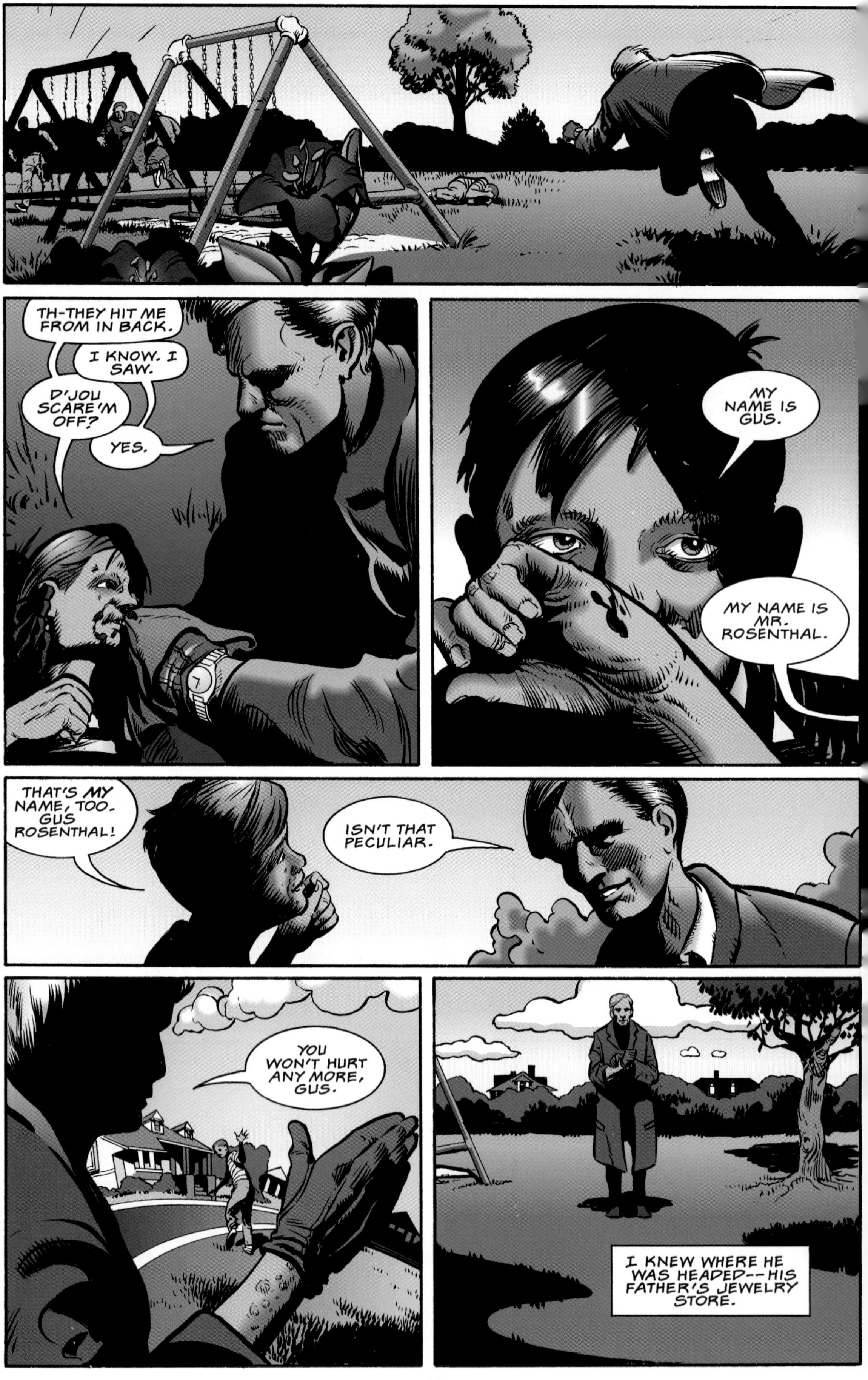
TH-THEY HIT ME FROM IN BACK.
I KNOW. I SAW.
D'JOU SCARE'M OFF?
YES.
MY NAME IS GUS.
MY NAME IS MR. ROSENTHAL.
THAT'S MY NAME, TOO-GUS ROSENTHAL!
ISN'T THAT PECULIAR.
YOU WON'T HURT ANY MORE, GUS.
I KNEW WHERE HE WAS HEADED--HIS FATHER'S JEWELRY STORE.

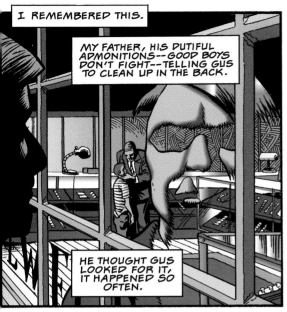

I REMEMBERED THIS.

MY FATHER, HIS DUTIFUL ADMONITIONS--GOOD BOYS DON'T FIGHT--TELLING GUS TO CLEAN UP IN THE BACK.

HE THOUGHT GUS LOOKED FOR IT, IT HAPPENED SO OFTEN.

I COULDN'T BLAME HIM. BUT THIS TIME, AT LEAST, I COULD SET MATTERS RIGHT.

MR. ROSENTHAL?

IT TOOK HIM A MOMENT, SO KNOTTED WITH WORRY WAS HE OVER ME--OVER GUS.

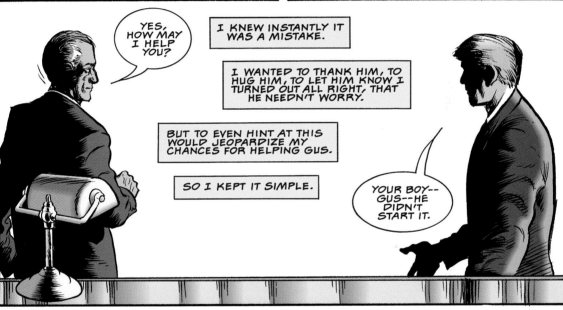

YES, HOW MAY I HELP YOU?

I KNEW INSTANTLY IT WAS A MISTAKE.

I WANTED TO THANK HIM, TO HUG HIM, TO LET HIM KNOW I TURNED OUT ALL RIGHT, THAT HE NEEDN'T WORRY.

BUT TO EVEN HINT AT THIS WOULD JEOPARDIZE MY CHANCES FOR HELPING GUS.

SO I KEPT IT SIMPLE.

YOUR BOY-- GUS--HE DIDN'T START IT.

I SAW THE FIGHT.

OTHER BOYS JUMPED GUS.

HE ONLY DEFENDED HIMSELF.

I THOUGHT YOU SHOULD KNOW.

I SEE--

THANK YOU... MR.--?

I GOT OUT. I ITCHED ALL OVER, KNOWING THERE WAS DANGER IN EVERY EXTRA WORD I MIGHT SAY.

I NOTICED A RASH ON MY WRIST.

WAIT!

POP, WHERE'S A TOWEL?

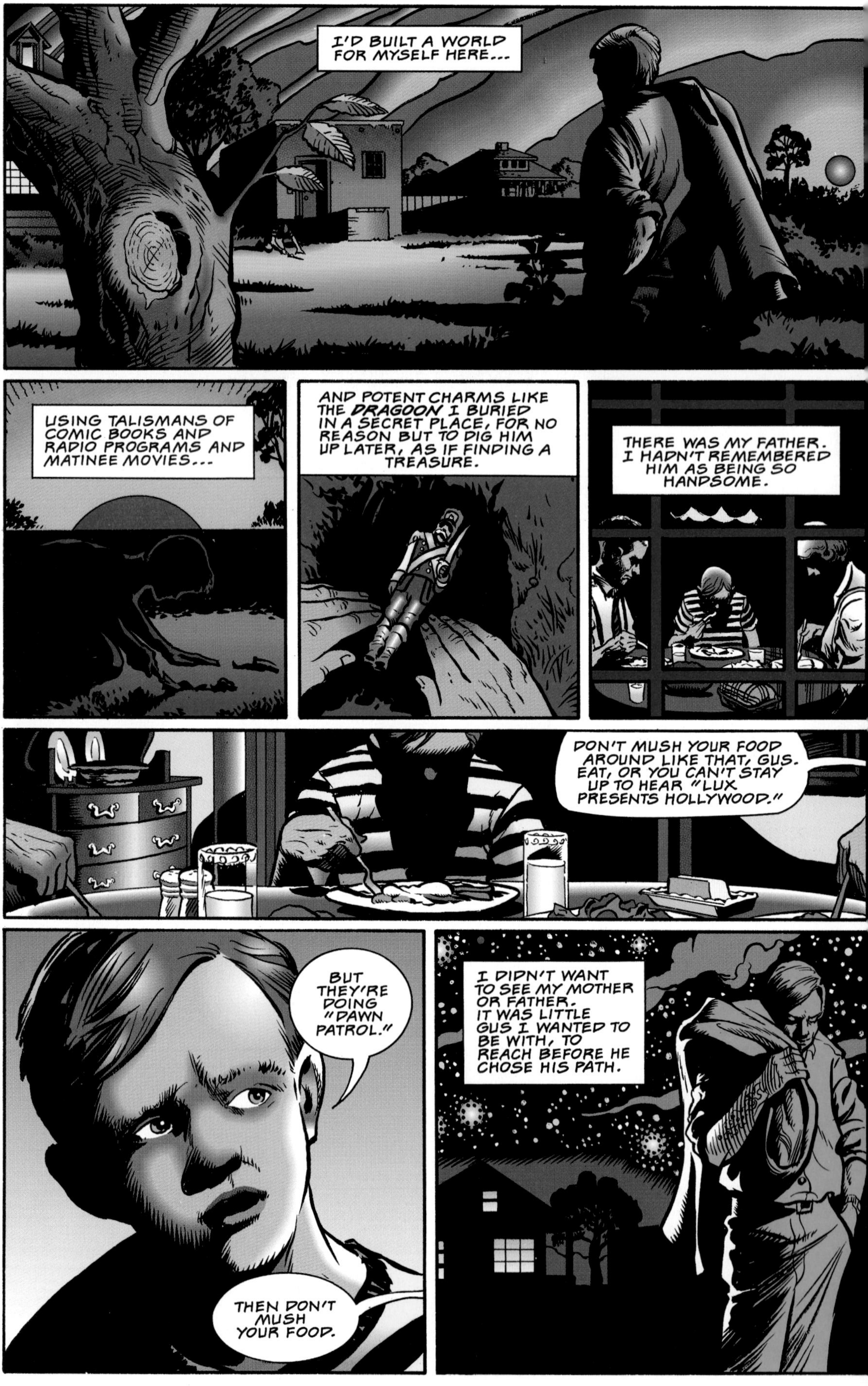
I'D BUILT A WORLD FOR MYSELF HERE...
USING TALISMANS OF COMIC BOOKS AND RADIO PROGRAMS AND MATINEE MOVIES...
AND POTENT CHARMS LIKE THE DRAGOON I BURIED IN A SECRET PLACE, FOR NO REASON BUT TO DIG HIM UP LATER, AS IF FINDING A TREASURE.
THERE WAS MY FATHER. I HADN'T REMEMBERED HIM AS BEING SO HANDSOME.
DON'T MUSH YOUR FOOD AROUND LIKE THAT, GUS. EAT, OR YOU CAN'T STAY UP TO HEAR "LUX PRESENTS HOLLYWOOD."
BUT THEY'RE DOING "DAWN PATROL."
THEN DON'T MUSH YOUR FOOD.
I DIDN'T WANT TO SEE MY MOTHER OR FATHER. IT WAS LITTLE GUS I WANTED TO BE WITH, TO REACH BEFORE HE CHOSE HIS PATH.

WHAT DO YOU WANT TO BE WHEN YOU GROW UP, GUS?

I DON'T KNOW. MAYBE I COULD DRAW COMIC BOOKS.

THERE'S A LOT OF MONEY TO BE MADE IN ART.

IT'S *FUN*, TOO, ISN'T IT?

I WAS EMBARRASSED. I'D THOUGHT FIRST OF MONEY; HE'D THOUGHT FIRST OF HAPPINESS.

THERE WAS STILL TIME TO MAKE HIM A MAN WHO WOULD THINK FIRST OF JOY, ALL THROUGH HIS LIFE.

MR. ROSENTHAL, WHY'D THEY CALL ME "ELEPHANT"?

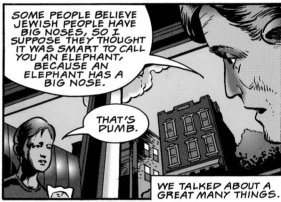

SOME PEOPLE BELIEVE JEWISH PEOPLE HAVE BIG NOSES, SO I SUPPOSE THEY THOUGHT IT WAS SMART TO CALL YOU AN ELEPHANT, BECAUSE AN ELEPHANT HAS A BIG NOSE.

THAT'S DUMB.

WE TALKED ABOUT A GREAT MANY THINGS.

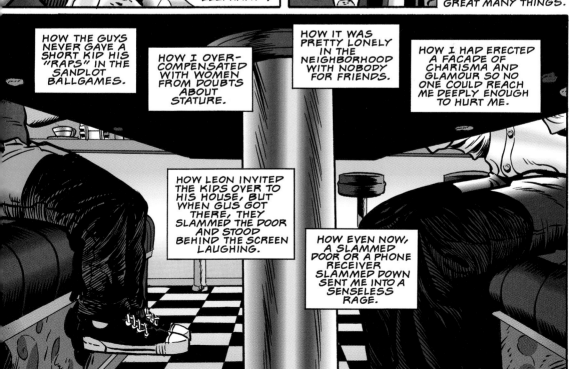

HOW THE GUYS NEVER GAVE A SHORT KID HIS "RAPS" IN THE SANDLOT BALLGAMES.

HOW I OVER-COMPENSATED WITH WOMEN FROM DOUBTS ABOUT STATURE.

HOW IT WAS PRETTY LONELY IN THE NEIGHBORHOOD WITH NOBODY FOR FRIENDS.

HOW I HAD ERECTED A FACADE OF CHARISMA AND GLAMOUR SO NO ONE COULD REACH ME DEEPLY ENOUGH TO HURT ME.

HOW LEON INVITED THE KIDS OVER TO HIS HOUSE, BUT WHEN GUS GOT THERE, THEY SLAMMED THE DOOR AND STOOD BEHIND THE SCREEN LAUGHING.

HOW EVEN NOW, A SLAMMED DOOR OR A PHONE RECEIVER SLAMMED DOWN SENT ME INTO A SENSELESS RAGE.

13

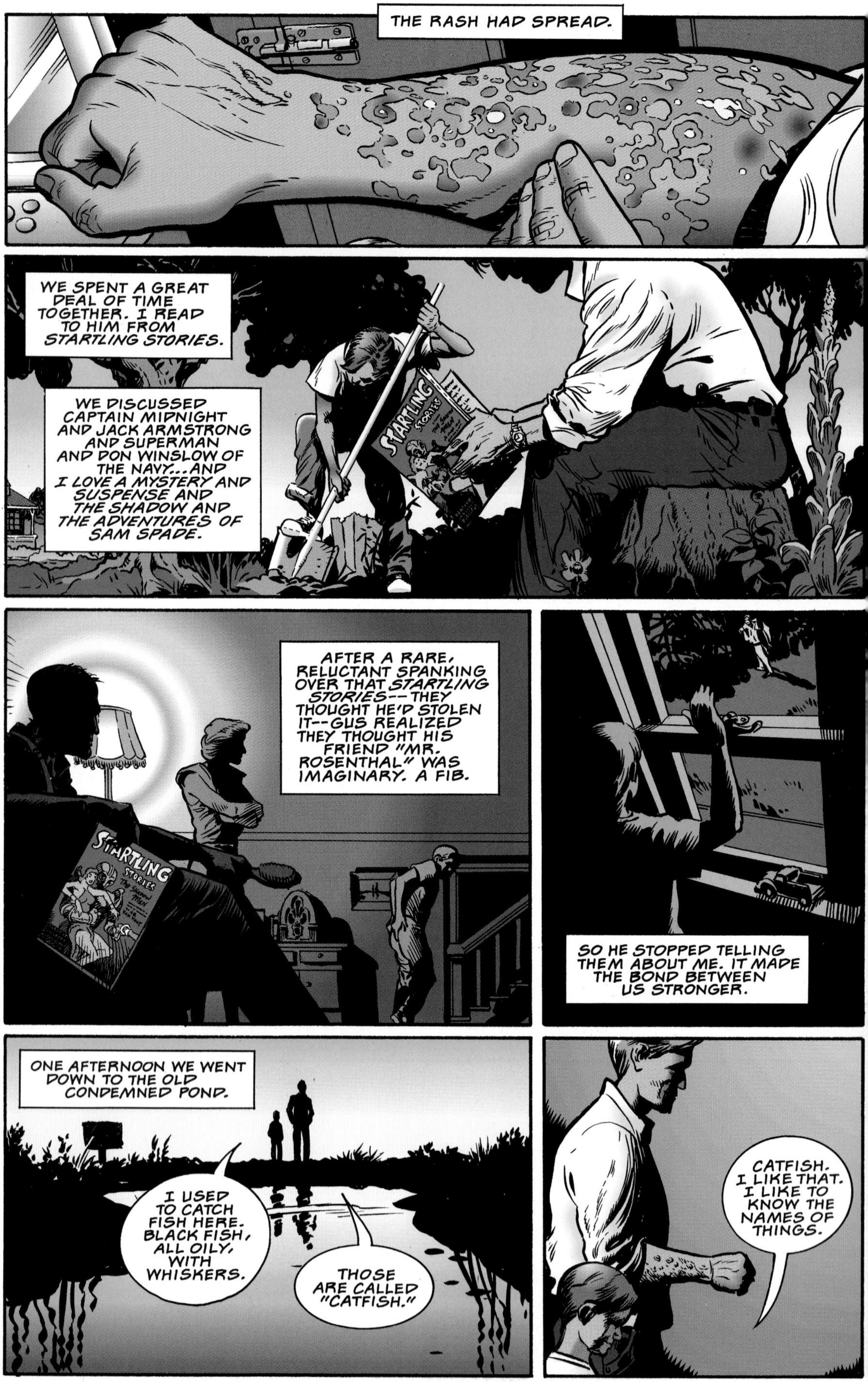
THE RASH HAD SPREAD.
WE SPENT A GREAT DEAL OF TIME TOGETHER. I READ TO HIM FROM STARTLING STORIES.
WE DISCUSSED CAPTAIN MIDNIGHT AND JACK ARMSTRONG AND SUPERMAN AND DON WINSLOW OF THE NAVY...AND I LOVE A MYSTERY AND SUSPENSE AND THE SHADOW AND THE ADVENTURES OF SAM SPADE.
STARTLING STORIES
AFTER A RARE, RELUCTANT SPANKING OVER THAT STARTLING STORIES--THEY THOUGHT HE'D STOLEN IT--GUS REALIZED THEY THOUGHT HIS FRIEND "MR. ROSENTHAL" WAS IMAGINARY. A FIB.
STARTLING STORIES
SO HE STOPPED TELLING THEM ABOUT ME. IT MADE THE BOND BETWEEN US STRONGER.
ONE AFTERNOON WE WENT DOWN TO THE OLD CONDEMNED POND.
I USED TO CATCH FISH HERE. BLACK FISH, ALL OILY, WITH WHISKERS.
THOSE ARE CALLED "CATFISH."
CATFISH. I LIKE THAT. I LIKE TO KNOW THE NAMES OF THINGS.

I TOLD HIM *THAT* WAS CALLED "NOMENCLATURE." HE LAUGHED TO KNOW THERE WAS A NAME FOR KNOWING NAMES.

HE WANTED TO KNOW ABOUT WHERE I'D BEEN, WHAT I'D DONE.

I RAN AWAY FROM HOME WHEN I WAS THIRTEEN, GUS.

WASN'T YOU HAPPY THERE?

WELL, YES AND NO. THEY LOVED ME, MY MOTHER AND FATHER. THEY REALLY DID.

THEY JUST DIDN'T UNDERSTAND WHAT I WAS ALL ABOUT.

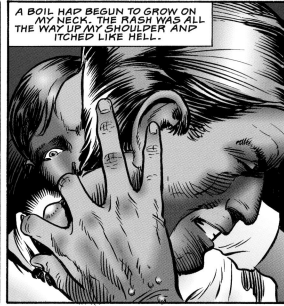

A BOIL HAD BEGUN TO GROW ON MY NECK. THE RASH WAS ALL THE WAY UP MY SHOULDER AND ITCHED LIKE HELL.

I TOLD HIM ABOUT JOINING THE CARNIVAL AND ABOUT MOLL DIPS AND CANNONS AND PAPER-HANGERS...

A CANNON'S A PICKPOCKET, AND A MOLL DIP IS A LADY PICKPOCKET, AND A PAPER-HANGER IS A FELLOW WHO WRITES BAD CHECKS, YOU SEE?

SO ONE NIGHT IN KANSAS CITY, ONE OF THESE CANNONS PICKED THE POCKET OF AN ASSISTANT DISTRICT ATTORNEY...

15

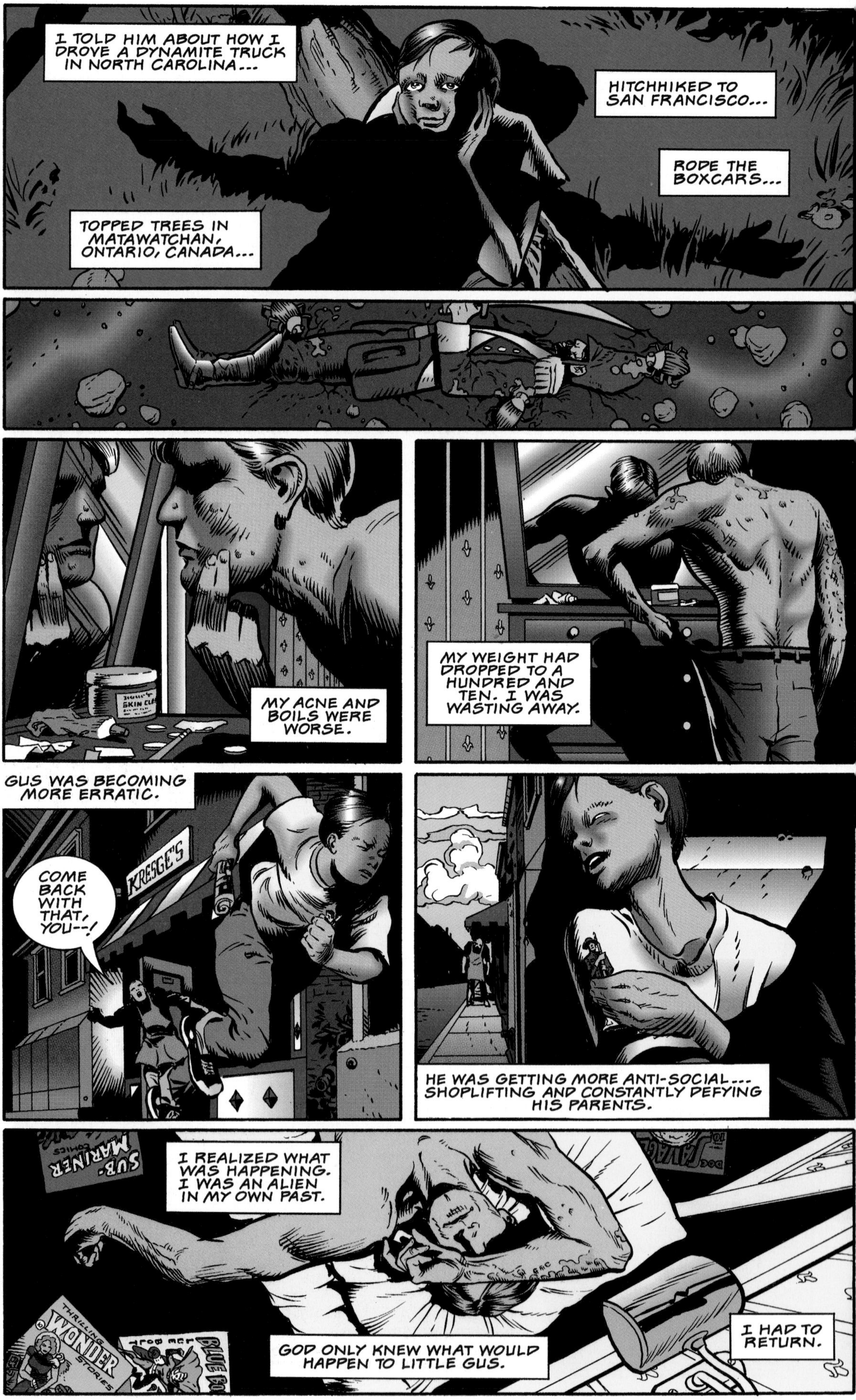
I TOLD HIM ABOUT HOW I DROVE A DYNAMITE TRUCK IN NORTH CAROLINA...
HITCHHIKED TO SAN FRANCISCO...
RODE THE BOXCARS...
TOPPED TREES IN MATAWATCHAN, ONTARIO, CANADA...
MY ACNE AND BOILS WERE WORSE.
MY WEIGHT HAD DROPPED TO A HUNDRED AND TEN. I WAS WASTING AWAY.
GUS WAS BECOMING MORE ERRATIC.
KRESGE'S
COME BACK WITH THAT, YOU--!
HE WAS GETTING MORE ANTI-SOCIAL... SHOPLIFTING AND CONSTANTLY DEFYING HIS PARENTS.
SUB-MARINER
I REALIZED WHAT WAS HAPPENING. I WAS AN ALIEN IN MY OWN PAST.
THRILLING WONDER STORIES
GOD ONLY KNEW WHAT WOULD HAPPEN TO LITTLE GUS.
I HAD TO RETURN.

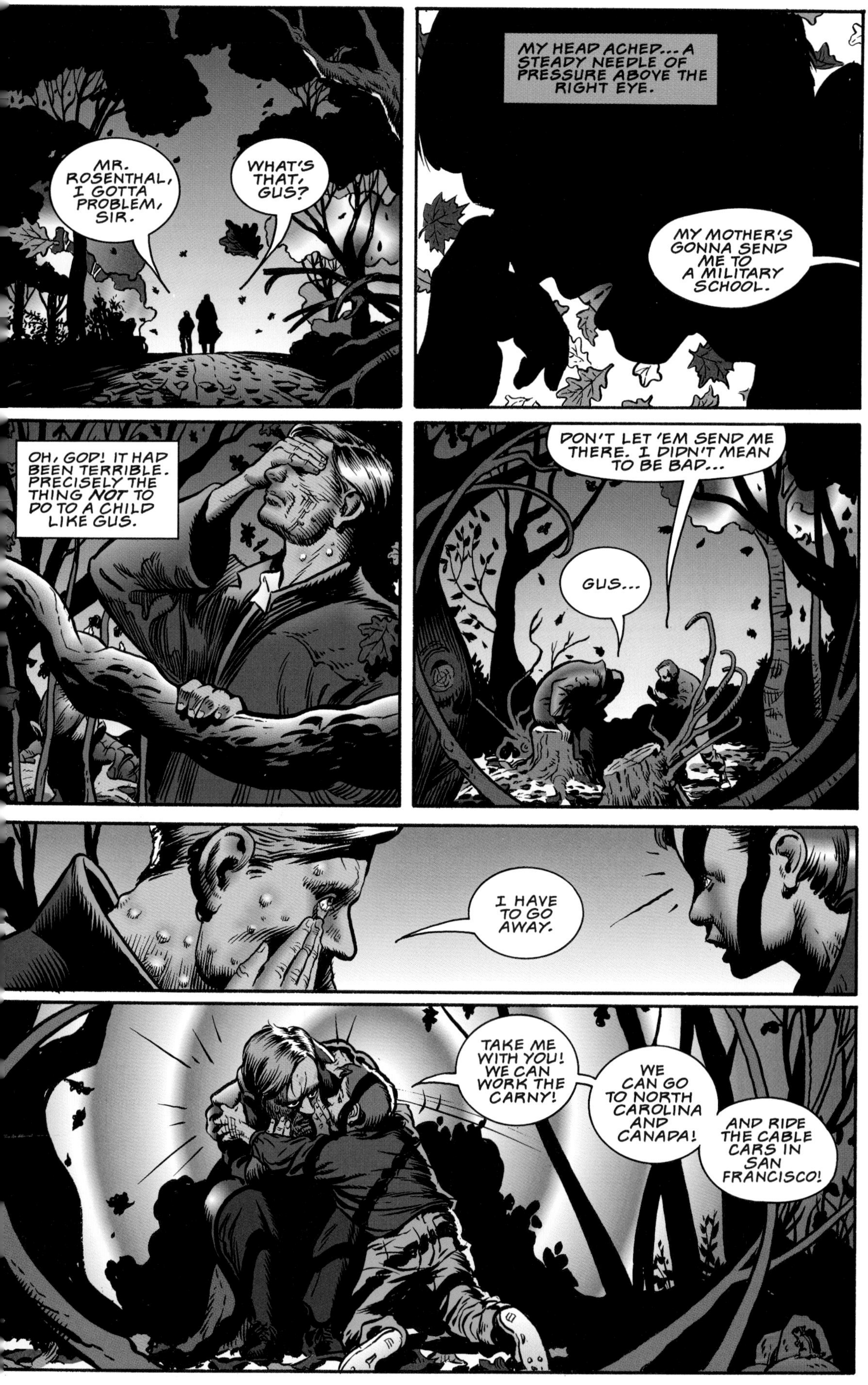
MR. ROSENTHAL, I GOTTA PROBLEM, SIR.
WHAT'S THAT, GUS?
MY HEAD ACHED... A STEADY NEEDLE OF PRESSURE ABOVE THE RIGHT EYE.
MY MOTHER'S GONNA SEND ME TO A MILITARY SCHOOL.
OH, GOD! IT HAD BEEN TERRIBLE. PRECISELY THE THING NOT TO DO TO A CHILD LIKE GUS.
DON'T LET 'EM SEND ME THERE. I DIDN'T MEAN TO BE BAD...
GUS...
I HAVE TO GO AWAY.
TAKE ME WITH YOU! WE CAN WORK THE CARNY!
WE CAN GO TO NORTH CAROLINA AND CANADA!
AND RIDE THE CABLE CARS IN SAN FRANCISCO!

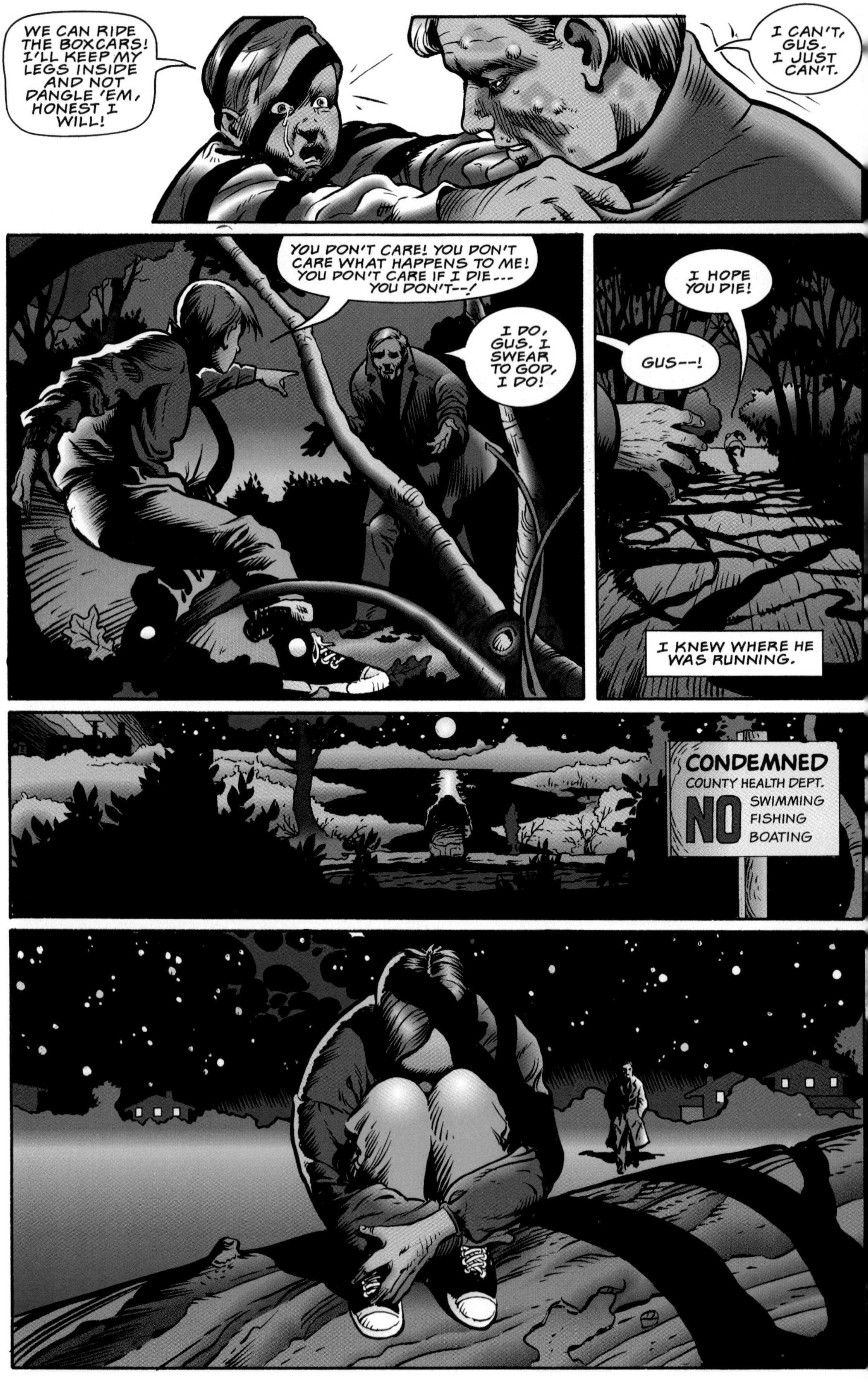
WE CAN RIDE THE BOXCARS! I'LL KEEP MY LEGS INSIDE AND NOT DANGLE 'EM, HONEST I WILL!
I CAN'T, GUS. I JUST CAN'T.
YOU DON'T CARE! YOU DON'T CARE WHAT HAPPENS TO ME! YOU DON'T CARE IF I DIE--- YOU DON'T--!
I DO, GUS. I SWEAR TO GOD, I DO!
I HOPE YOU DIE!
GUS--!
I KNEW WHERE HE WAS RUNNING.
CONDEMNED
COUNTY HEALTH DEPT.
NO SWIMMING FISHING BOATING

HEY. HEY, LITTLE GUS.

DON'T GO, PLEASE DON'T GO, PLEASE TAKE ME WITH YOU, PLEASE DON'T LEAVE ME HERE ALONE...

IF YOU LEAVE ME I'LL DIE. I WILL!

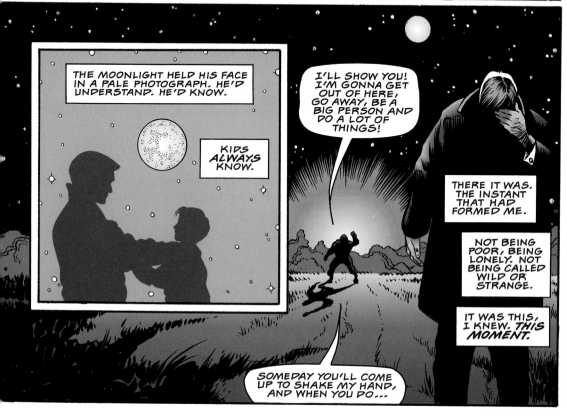

THE MOONLIGHT HELD HIS FACE IN A PALE PHOTOGRAPH. HE'D UNDERSTAND. HE'D KNOW.

KIDS ALWAYS KNOW.

I'LL SHOW YOU! I'M GONNA GET OUT OF HERE, GO AWAY, BE A BIG PERSON AND DO A LOT OF THINGS!

THERE IT WAS. THE INSTANT THAT HAD FORMED ME.

NOT BEING POOR, BEING LONELY. NOT BEING CALLED WILD OR STRANGE.

IT WAS THIS, I KNEW. THIS MOMENT.

SOMEDAY YOU'LL COME UP TO SHAKE MY HAND, AND WHEN YOU DO...

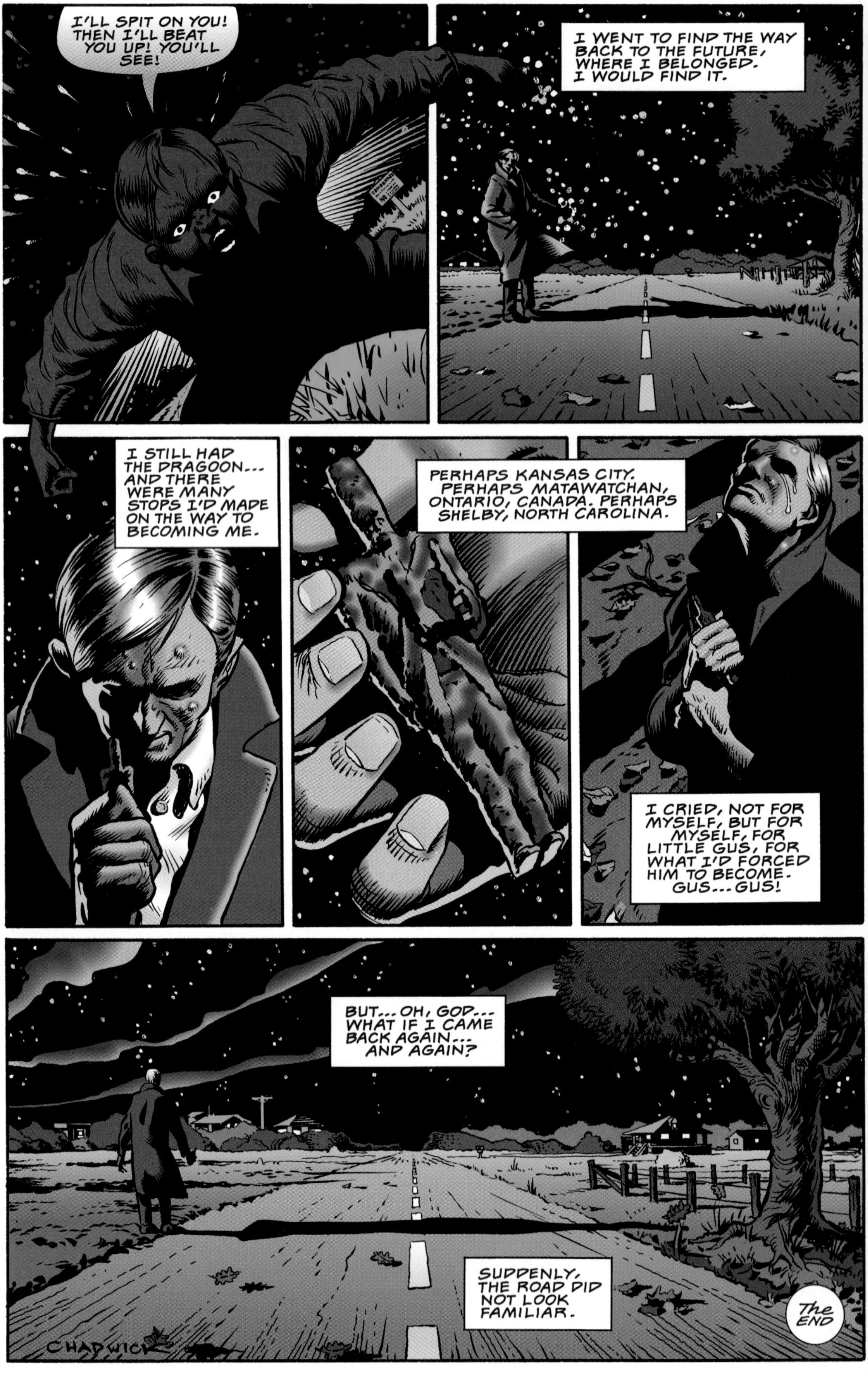
I'LL SPIT ON YOU! THEN I'LL BEAT YOU UP! YOU'LL SEE!
I WENT TO FIND THE WAY BACK TO THE FUTURE, WHERE I BELONGED. I WOULD FIND IT.
I STILL HAD THE DRAGOON... AND THERE WERE MANY STOPS I'D MADE ON THE WAY TO BECOMING ME.
PERHAPS KANSAS CITY. PERHAPS MATAWATCHAN, ONTARIO, CANADA. PERHAPS SHELBY, NORTH CAROLINA.
I CRIED, NOT FOR MYSELF, BUT FOR MYSELF, FOR LITTLE GUS, FOR WHAT I'D FORCED HIM TO BECOME. GUS... GUS!
BUT... OH, GOD... WHAT IF I CAME BACK AGAIN... AND AGAIN?
SUDDENLY, THE ROAD DID NOT LOOK FAMILIAR.
The END
CHADWICK

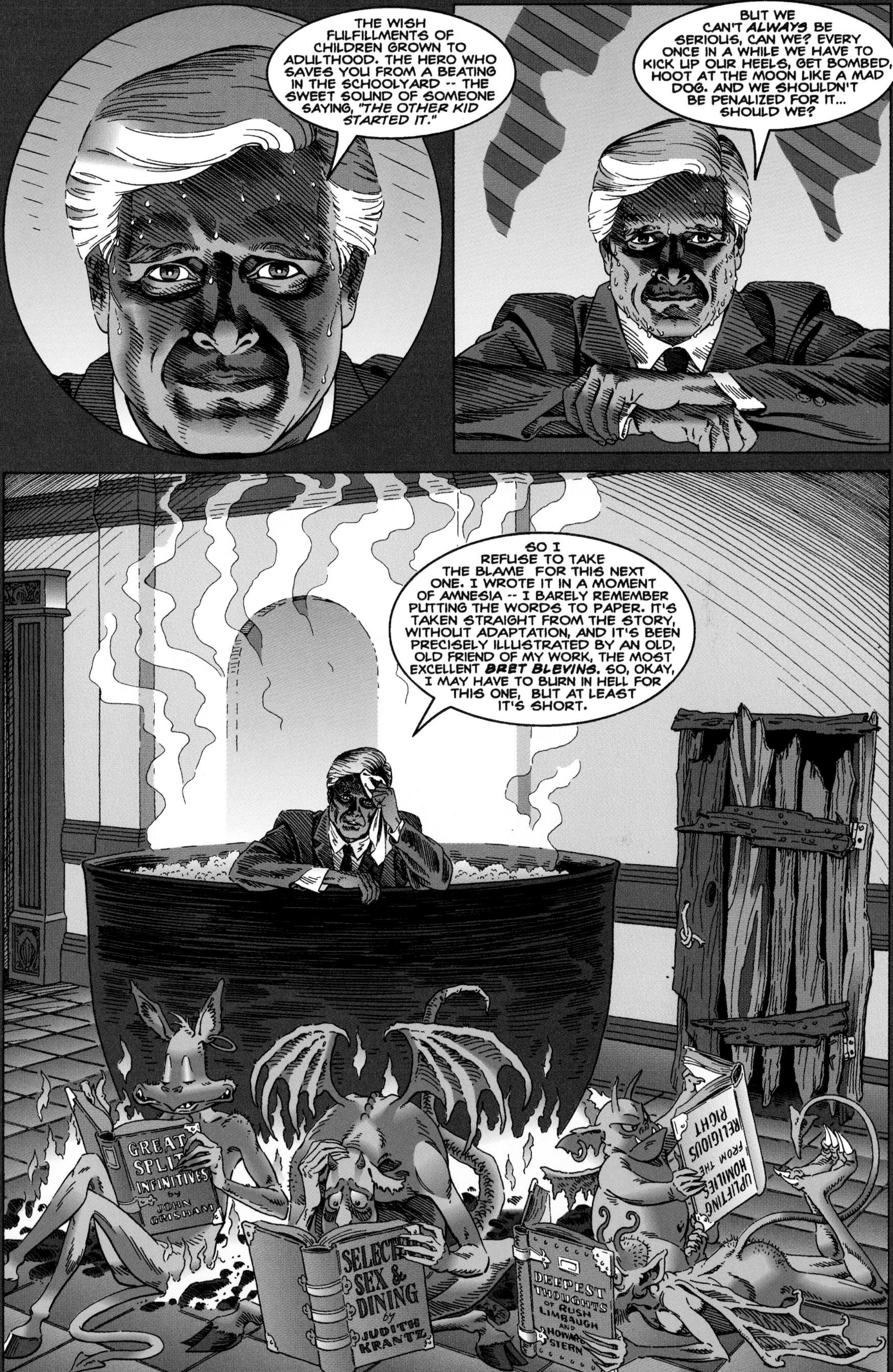

THE WISH FULFILLMENTS OF CHILDREN GROWN TO ADULTHOOD. THE HERO WHO SAVES YOU FROM A BEATING IN THE SCHOOLYARD -- THE SWEET SOUND OF SOMEONE SAYING, "THE OTHER KID STARTED IT."
BUT WE CAN'T ALWAYS BE SERIOUS, CAN WE? EVERY ONCE IN A WHILE WE HAVE TO KICK UP OUR HEELS, GET BOMBED, HOOT AT THE MOON LIKE A MAD DOG. AND WE SHOULDN'T BE PENALIZED FOR IT... SHOULD WE?
SO I REFUSE TO TAKE THE BLAME FOR THIS NEXT ONE. I WROTE IT IN A MOMENT OF AMNESIA -- I BARELY REMEMBER PUTTING THE WORDS TO PAPER. IT'S TAKEN STRAIGHT FROM THE STORY, WITHOUT ADAPTATION, AND IT'S BEEN PRECISELY ILLUSTRATED BY AN OLD, OLD FRIEND OF MY WORK, THE MOST EXCELLENT BRET BLEVINS. SO, OKAY, I MAY HAVE TO BURN IN HELL FOR THIS ONE, BUT AT LEAST IT'S SHORT.
GREAT SPLIT INFINITIVES by JOHN GRISHAM
SELECTE SEX & DINING by JUDITH KRANTZ
DEEPEST THOUGHTS OF RUSH LIMBAUGH AND HOWAR STERN
UPLIFTING HOMILIES FROM THE RELIGIOUS RIGHT

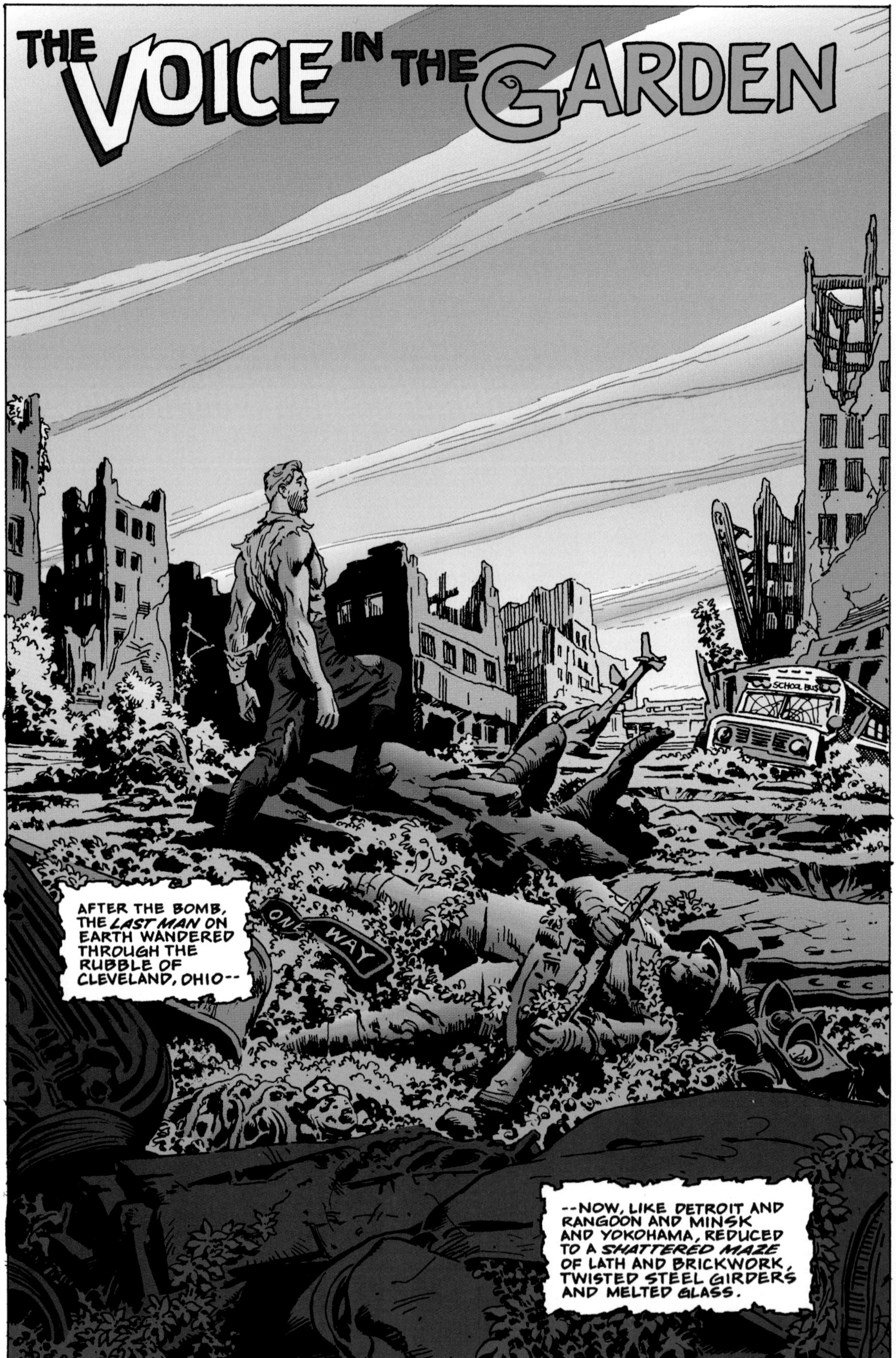
THE VOICE IN THE GARDEN
AFTER THE BOMB, THE LAST MAN ON EARTH WANDERED THROUGH THE RUBBLE OF CLEVELAND, OHIO--
ONE WAY
SCHOOL BUS
--NOW, LIKE DETROIT AND RANGOON AND MINSK AND YOKOHAMA, REDUCED TO A SHATTERED MAZE OF LATH AND BRICKWORK, TWISTED STEEL GIRDERS AND MELTED GLASS.

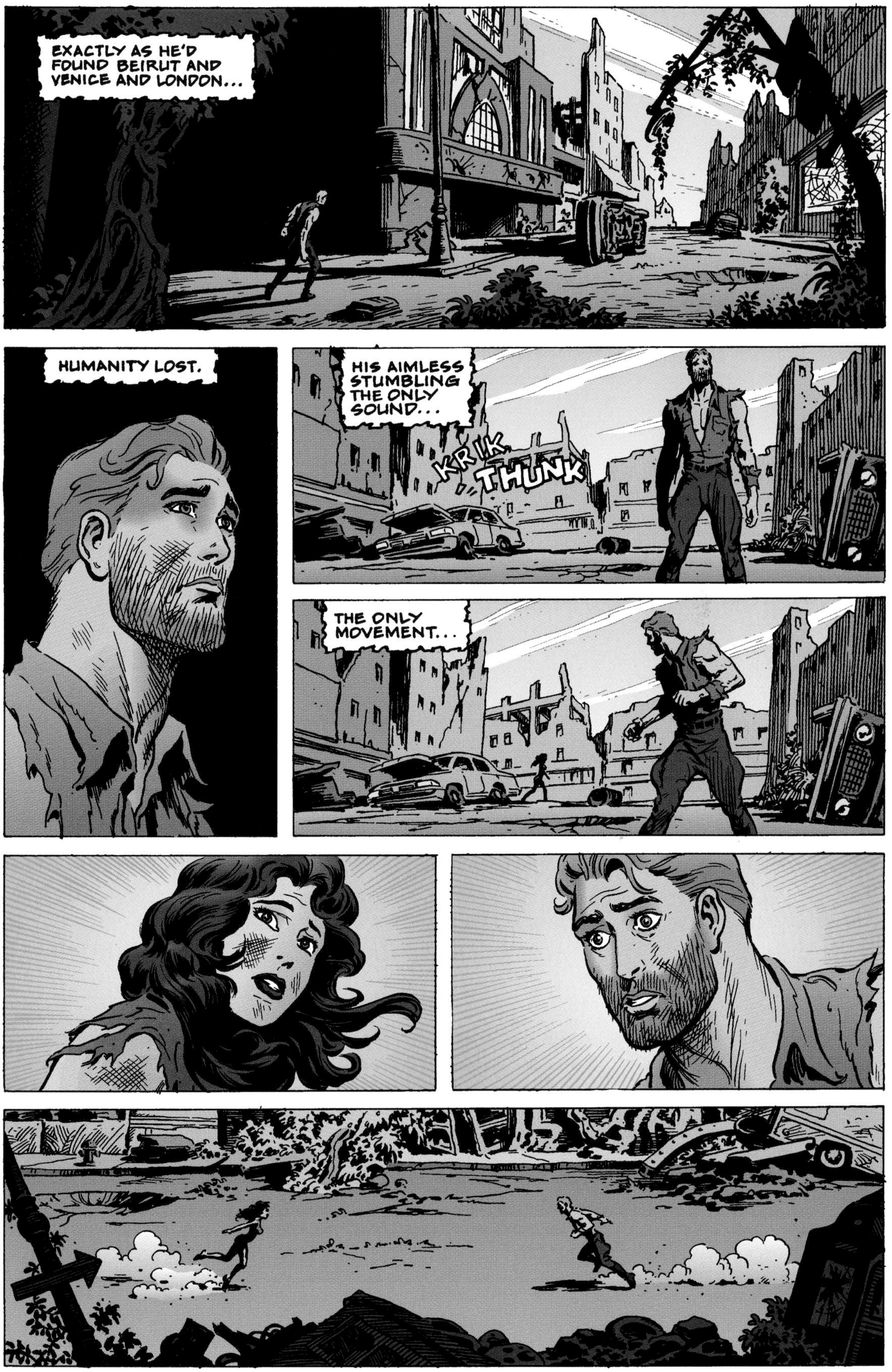
EXACTLY AS HE'D FOUND BEIRUT AND VENICE AND LONDON...
HUMANITY LOST.
HIS AIMLESS STUMBLING THE ONLY SOUND...
KRIK
THUNK
THE ONLY MOVEMENT...

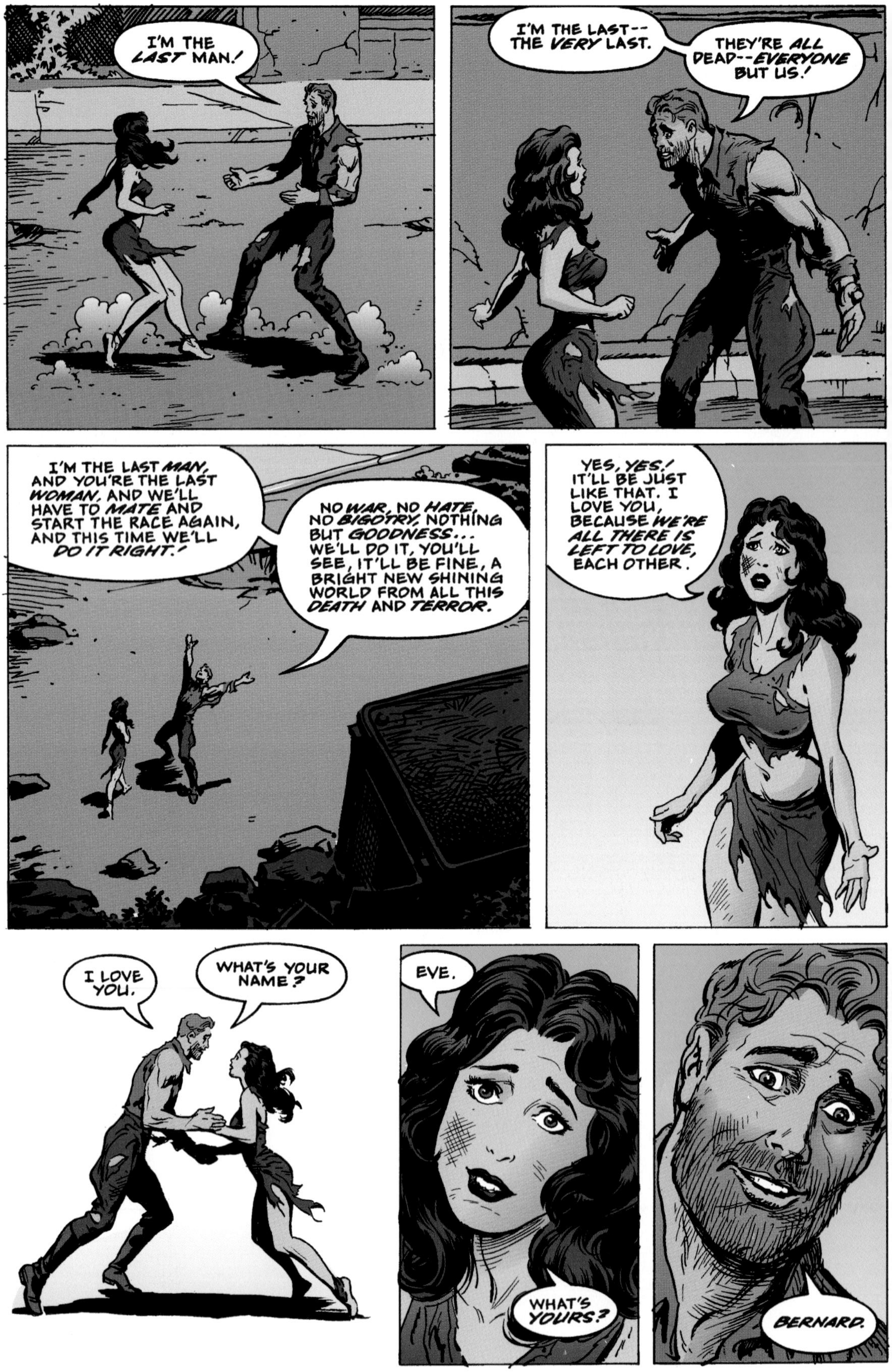
I'M THE LAST MAN.!
I'M THE LAST-- THE VERY LAST.
THEY'RE ALL DEAD--EVERYONE BUT US.!
I'M THE LAST MAN, AND YOU'RE THE LAST WOMAN, AND WE'LL HAVE TO MATE AND START THE RACE AGAIN, AND THIS TIME WE'LL DO IT RIGHT.!
NO WAR, NO HATE, NO BIGOTRY, NOTHING BUT GOODNESS... WE'LL DO IT, YOU'LL SEE, IT'LL BE FINE, A BRIGHT NEW SHINING WORLD FROM ALL THIS DEATH AND TERROR.
YES, YES.! IT'LL BE JUST LIKE THAT. I LOVE YOU, BECAUSE WE'RE ALL THERE IS LEFT TO LOVE, EACH OTHER.
I LOVE YOU.
WHAT'S YOUR NAME?
EVE.
WHAT'S YOURS?
BERNARD.

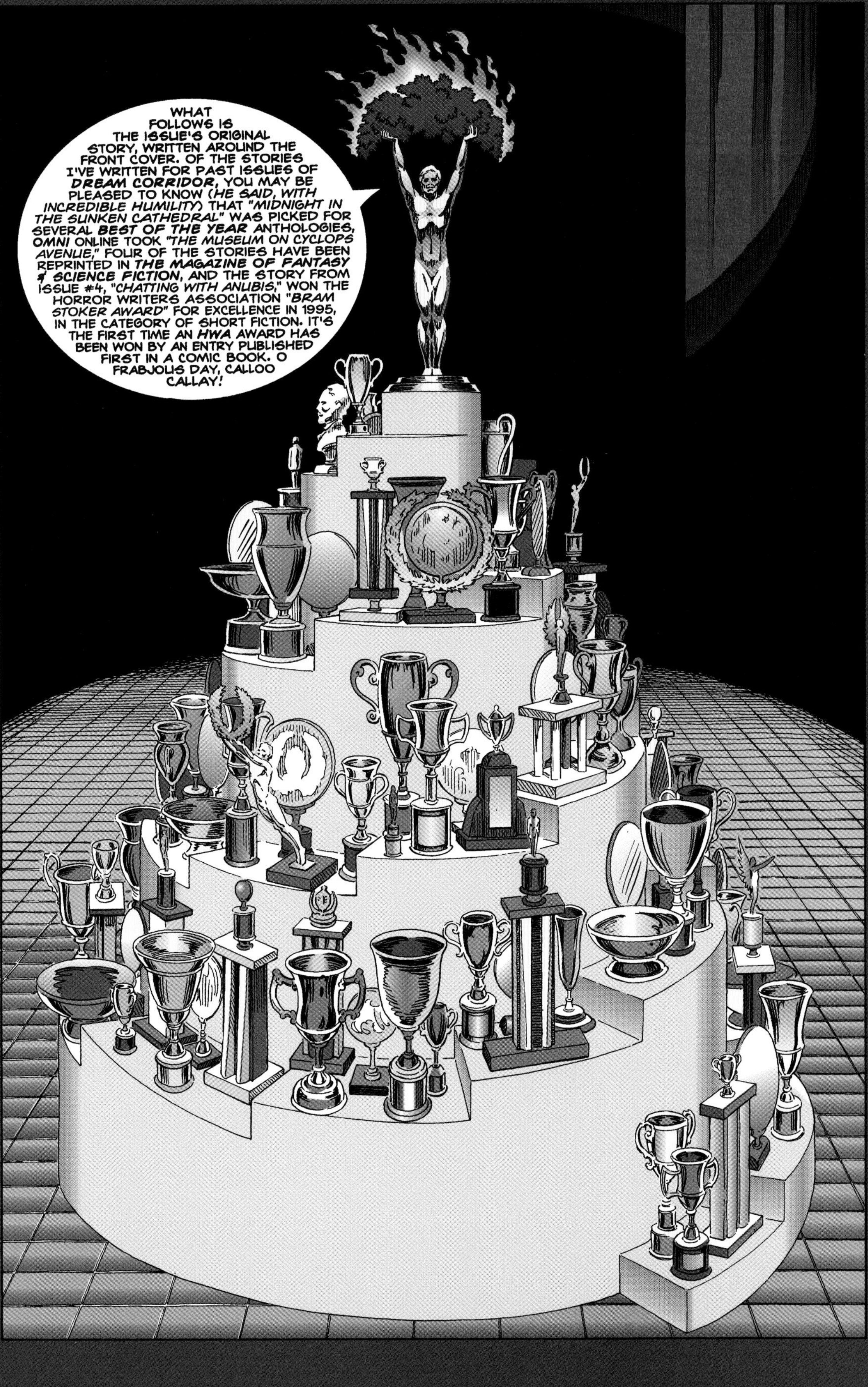
WHAT FOLLOWS IS THE ISSUE'S ORIGINAL STORY, WRITTEN AROUND THE FRONT COVER. OF THE STORIES I'VE WRITTEN FOR PAST ISSUES OF ***DREAM CORRIDOR***, YOU MAY BE PLEASED TO KNOW (*HE SAID, WITH INCREDIBLE HUMILITY*) THAT "*MIDNIGHT IN THE SUNKEN CATHEDRAL*" WAS PICKED FOR SEVERAL ***BEST OF THE YEAR*** ANTHOLOGIES, *OMNI* ONLINE TOOK "*THE MUSEUM ON CYCLOPS AVENUE*," FOUR OF THE STORIES HAVE BEEN REPRINTED IN ***THE MAGAZINE OF FANTASY & SCIENCE FICTION***, AND THE STORY FROM ISSUE #4, "*CHATTING WITH ANUBIS*," WON THE HORROR WRITERS ASSOCIATION "*BRAM STOKER AWARD*" FOR EXCELLENCE IN 1995, IN THE CATEGORY OF SHORT FICTION. IT'S THE FIRST TIME AN *HWA* AWARD HAS BEEN WON BY AN ENTRY PUBLISHED FIRST IN A COMIC BOOK. O FRABJOUS DAY, CALLOO CALLAY!

The story behind the cover:

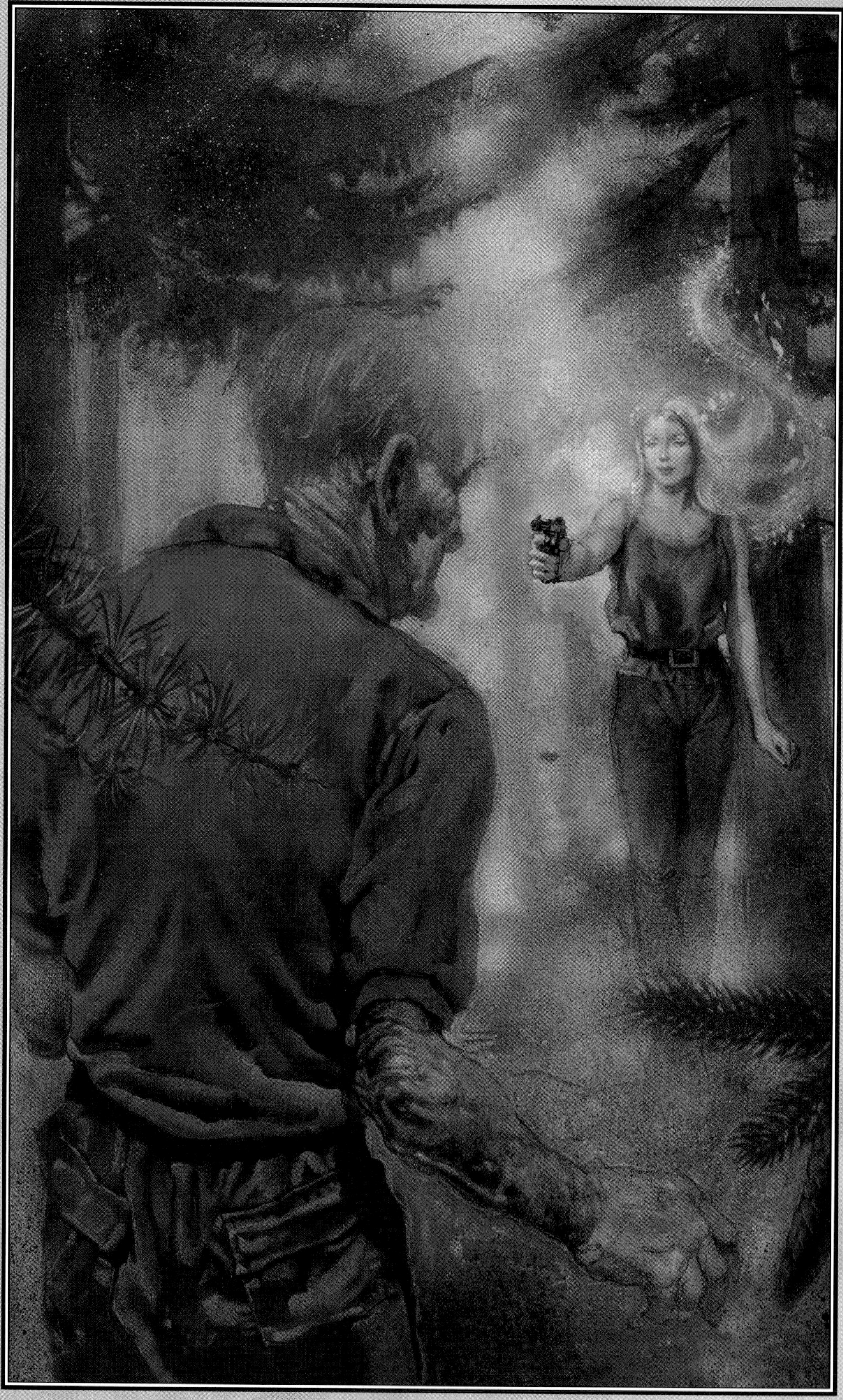

Painting by Terese Nielsen

HARLAN ELLISON

THE LINGERING SCENT OF WOODSMOKE

"Don't get your shorts in a twist," she said, leveling the Walther 9mm parabellum's four-and-a-half-inch barrel at a spot just south of the waistband of his woodland green walking shorts. "Stand totally, absolutely still as a weed and I won't have to blow you in half."

Near sundown, they stood facing each other in a small forest stand of spruce and Polish larch in the Oświęcim basin of southern Poland. Even under the smothering canopy of woven branches, they could hear the Vistula rushing fast and deep toward Czechoslovakia; they could smell the high Carpathians just to the north. She had stepped suddenly from behind a thick-trunked fir and ordered him to stand still. Even in the dimming light that filtered through from above, he could see she was extraordinarily beautiful, with exotic, almost Eurasian planes sculpting her features. The thick, filtered falling light gave everything a deep green tone, even her skin; her wide, green eyes; the imposing weapon in her hand.

"You're Ernst Koegel," she said to the old man. She spoke in German, with possibly a Bavarian crispness.

"My name is Dário de Queluz. I am from São Paulo. That is in Brazil. I walk here on a walking tour of Eastern Europe."

"I *know* where São Paulo is, there are some luxurious jungles nearby; and if you move like that again, I will most certainly shorten you *and* your shorts."

"So you are some lowlife Polish thug lying in wait for decent tourists? You can have the few thousand zloty I'm carrying. It is sad for you that my money is back in my hotel room in Kraków." He started to reach into one of the gusseted front pockets of his shorts, with the sound of Velcro. She waggled the barrel of the Walther and shook her head.

"You are Ernst Koegel, you're German, you were nineteen years old in 1944, when you worked in this area, and we've been waiting for you for fifty years."

"Waiting here? What if I had not decided to take this little journey? And you have my name wrong."

"Here; in the Amazon rain forest; in a woodland in upstate New York; anywhere your foot would tread among the trees. And don't try to bluff, old man: I can smell the lingering scent of woodsmoke on you."

"Take my money and let me go. I want to move."

"You stand still. I'm not a robber. I'm here to make you pay for killing my people. You worked just a half mile from here. In your language it was called Auschwitz. You worked with Mengele. You were in charge of stoking the great furnaces. Koegel, young Ernst Koegel, youngest SS officer in the death block, beloved of Dr. Mengele. When he fled, you went with him. Now you've come back, and we've been waiting."

The old man chuckled. Nothing could touch him. He had lived well. Even if she shot him now, he had lived well. "So," he said, smirking, "just another renegade Daughter of Esther, one of the *Juden* who managed to slip through."

"A Jew?" she said. "No, I'm not a Jew."

"We were disposing of twelve thousand a *day*, and I fed the furnaces. So do your worst, little green-faced kike."

"I tell you I'm not one of those poor unfortunates. My people you fed into the furnaces weren't the Jews. We are the forest people . . . and we wait for the last of you who used chain saws and cut down our families and sliced them into convenient sections and fed them into the furnaces. We can still smell the woodsmoke on you."

"You are crazier than most of them. But still you need the gun, that fine German-made weapon."

"Oh, this," she said, and let the Walther drop to her side. "I only needed this to keep you still long enough for my sisters to caress you properly."

And she smiled at him, and he realized that he no longer *could* move. He looked down, the old man who had run from this place half a century earlier, and he saw that the roots had already slithered up over his hiking boots, over his bare shins, up over his handsome, woodland green cargo shorts, and bark was already beginning to form around his waist.

He screamed once, a short sharp sound, because she was still smiling her deep green smile at him. And as the tree grew around him, the dryad dimpled prettily and said, "You should live, oh, I should say, two or three hundred years like this. The winters are rough, but you'll like the spring, and the smell of woodsmoke. That is, unless parasites infest you. Welcome to the neighborhood, cousin Ernst." ❏

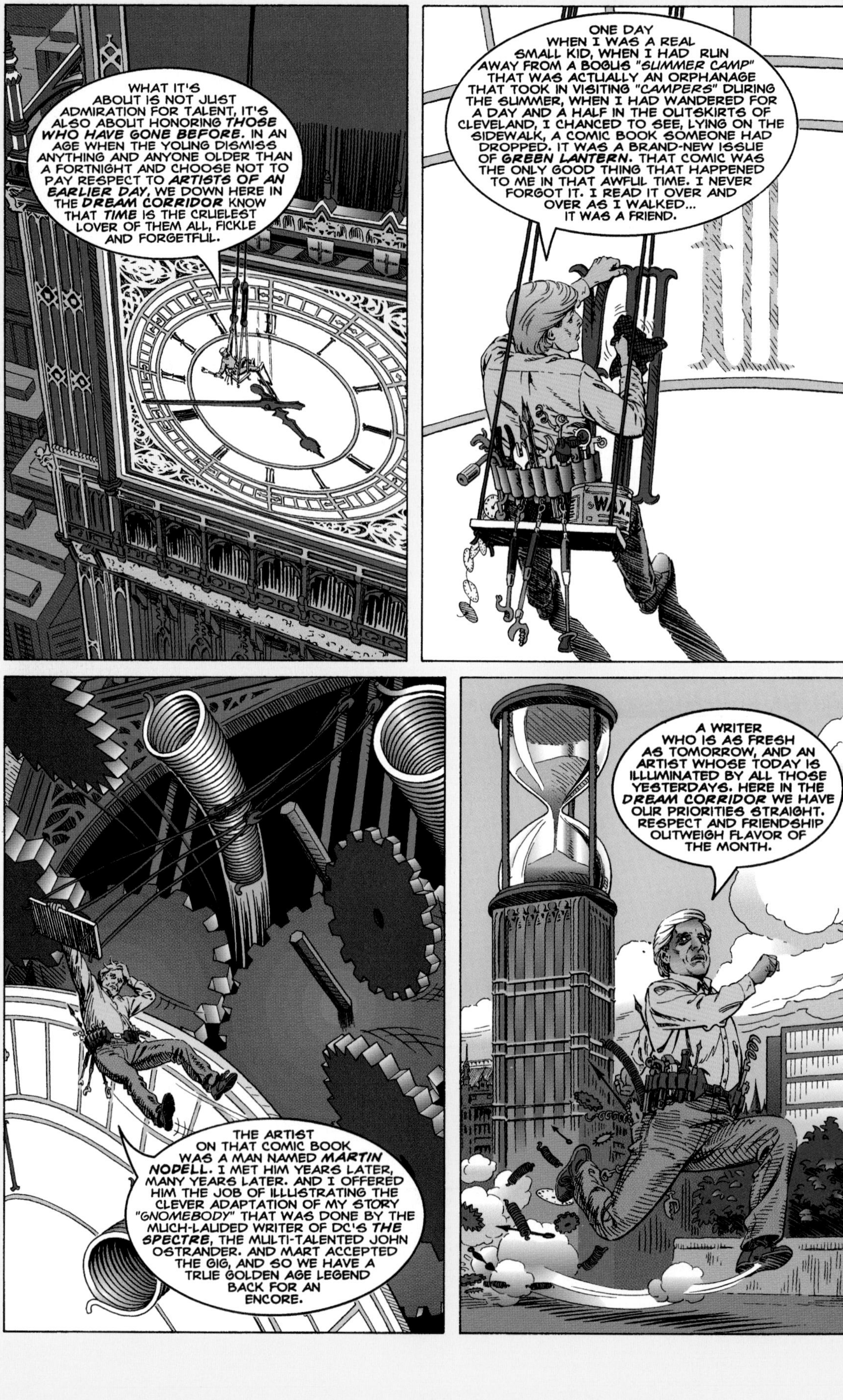
WHAT IT'S ABOUT IS NOT JUST ADMIRATION FOR TALENT, IT'S ALSO ABOUT HONORING *THOSE WHO HAVE GONE BEFORE*. IN AN AGE WHEN THE YOUNG DISMISS ANYTHING AND ANYONE OLDER THAN A FORTNIGHT AND CHOOSE NOT TO PAY RESPECT TO *ARTISTS OF AN EARLIER DAY*, WE DOWN HERE IN THE *DREAM CORRIDOR* KNOW THAT *TIME* IS THE CRUELEST LOVER OF THEM ALL, FICKLE AND FORGETFUL.
ONE DAY WHEN I WAS A REAL SMALL KID, WHEN I HAD RUN AWAY FROM A BOGUS *"SUMMER CAMP"* THAT WAS ACTUALLY AN ORPHANAGE THAT TOOK IN VISITING *"CAMPERS"* DURING THE SUMMER, WHEN I HAD WANDERED FOR A DAY AND A HALF IN THE OUTSKIRTS OF CLEVELAND, I CHANCED TO SEE, LYING ON THE SIDEWALK, A COMIC BOOK SOMEONE HAD DROPPED. IT WAS A BRAND-NEW ISSUE OF *GREEN LANTERN*. THAT COMIC WAS THE ONLY GOOD THING THAT HAPPENED TO ME IN THAT AWFUL TIME. I NEVER FORGOT IT. I READ IT OVER AND OVER AS I WALKED... IT WAS A FRIEND.
WAX
THE ARTIST ON THAT COMIC BOOK WAS A MAN NAMED *MARTIN NODELL*. I MET HIM YEARS LATER, MANY YEARS LATER. AND I OFFERED HIM THE JOB OF ILLUSTRATING THE CLEVER ADAPTATION OF MY STORY *"GNOMEBODY"* THAT WAS DONE BY THE MUCH-LAUDED WRITER OF DC'S *THE SPECTRE*, THE MULTI-TALENTED JOHN OSTRANDER. AND MART ACCEPTED THE GIG, AND SO WE HAVE A TRUE GOLDEN AGE LEGEND BACK FOR AN ENCORE.
A WRITER WHO IS AS FRESH AS TOMORROW, AND AN ARTIST WHOSE TODAY IS ILLUMINATED BY ALL THOSE YESTERDAYS. HERE IN THE *DREAM CORRIDOR* WE HAVE OUR PRIORITIES STRAIGHT. RESPECT AND FRIENDSHIP OUTWEIGH FLAVOR OF THE MONTH.

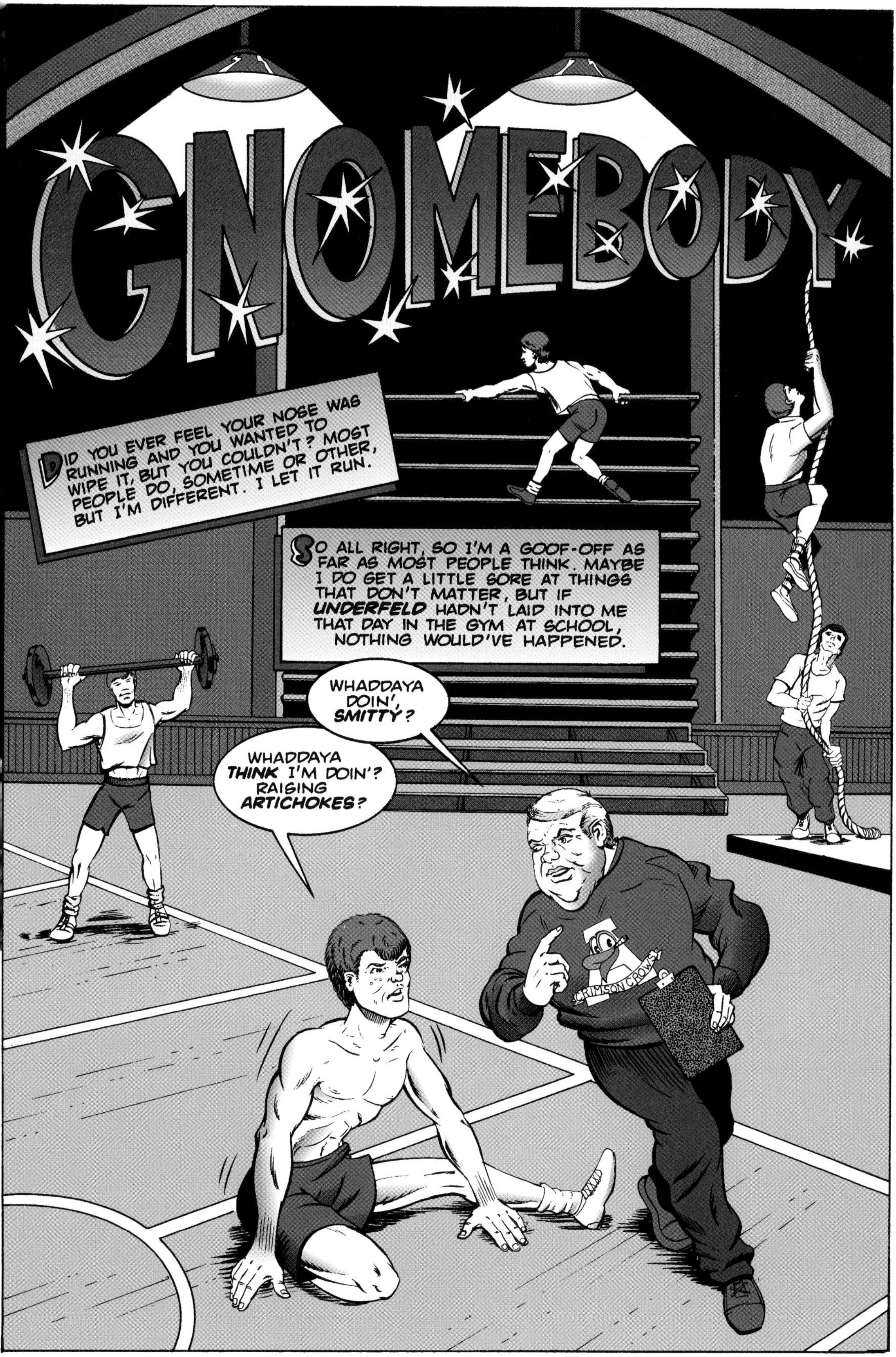
GNOMEBODY
DID YOU EVER FEEL YOUR NOSE WAS RUNNING AND YOU WANTED TO WIPE IT, BUT YOU COULDN'T? MOST PEOPLE DO, SOMETIME OR OTHER, BUT I'M DIFFERENT. I LET IT RUN.
SO ALL RIGHT, SO I'M A GOOF-OFF AS FAR AS MOST PEOPLE THINK. MAYBE I DO GET A LITTLE SORE AT THINGS THAT DON'T MATTER, BUT IF UNDERFELD HADN'T LAID INTO ME THAT DAY IN THE GYM AT SCHOOL, NOTHING WOULD'VE HAPPENED.
WHADDAYA DOIN', SMITTY?
WHADDAYA THINK I'M DOIN'? RAISING ARTICHOKES?
CRIMSON CROWS

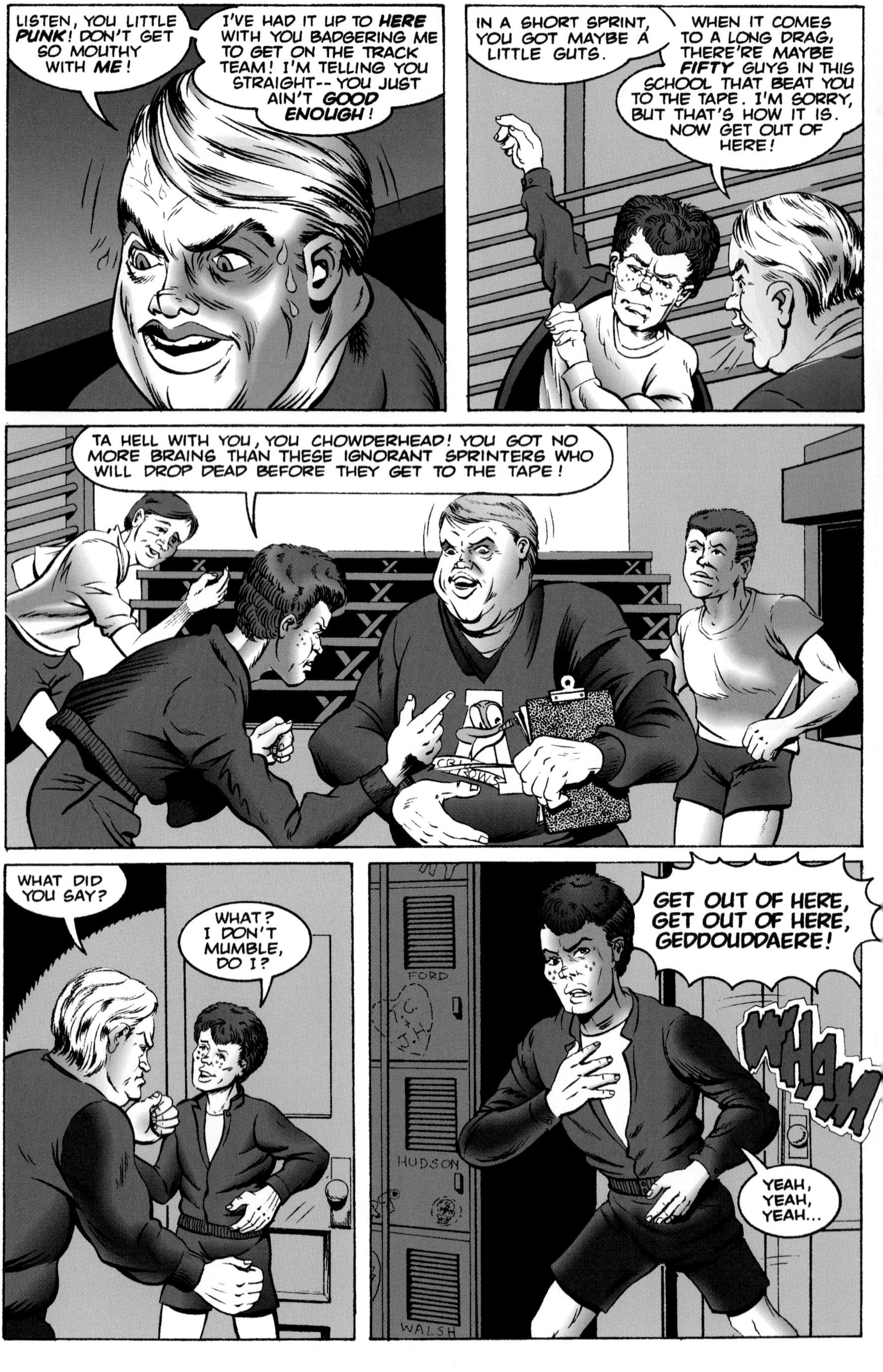
LISTEN, YOU LITTLE PUNK! DON'T GET SO MOUTHY WITH ME!
I'VE HAD IT UP TO HERE WITH YOU BADGERING ME TO GET ON THE TRACK TEAM! I'M TELLING YOU STRAIGHT-- YOU JUST AIN'T GOOD ENOUGH!
IN A SHORT SPRINT, YOU GOT MAYBE A LITTLE GUTS.
WHEN IT COMES TO A LONG DRAG, THERE'RE MAYBE FIFTY GUYS IN THIS SCHOOL THAT BEAT YOU TO THE TAPE. I'M SORRY, BUT THAT'S HOW IT IS. NOW GET OUT OF HERE!
TA HELL WITH YOU, YOU CHOWDERHEAD! YOU GOT NO MORE BRAINS THAN THESE IGNORANT SPRINTERS WHO WILL DROP DEAD BEFORE THEY GET TO THE TAPE!
WHAT DID YOU SAY?
WHAT? I DON'T MUMBLE, DO I?
GET OUT OF HERE, GET OUT OF HERE, GEDDOUDDAERE!
WHAM
YEAH, YEAH, YEAH...
FORD
HUDSON
WALSH

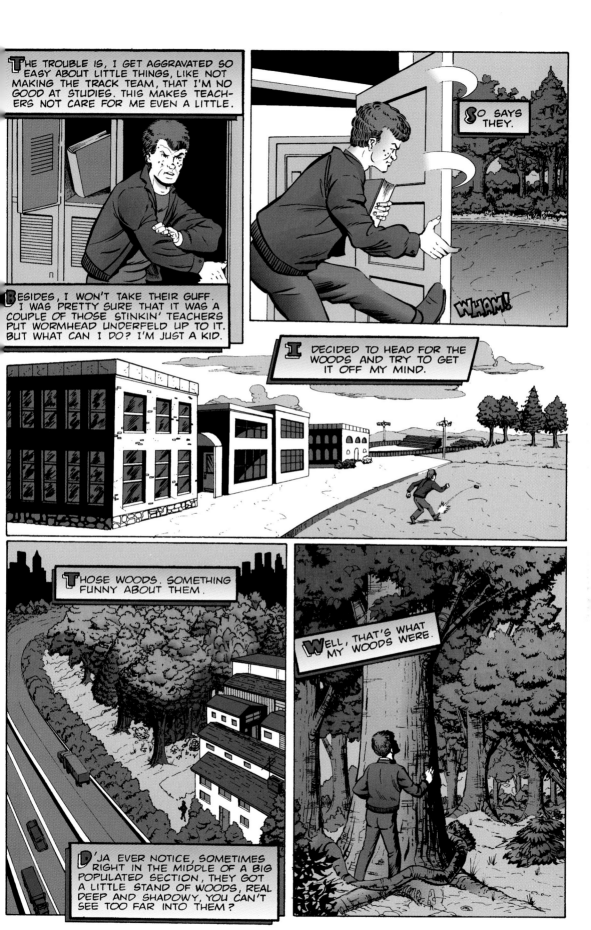

THE TROUBLE IS, I GET AGGRAVATED SO EASY ABOUT LITTLE THINGS, LIKE NOT MAKING THE TRACK TEAM, THAT I'M NO GOOD AT STUDIES. THIS MAKES TEACHERS NOT CARE FOR ME EVEN A LITTLE.

SO SAYS THEY.

BESIDES, I WON'T TAKE THEIR GUFF. I WAS PRETTY SURE THAT IT WAS A COUPLE OF THOSE STINKIN' TEACHERS PUT WORMHEAD UNDERFELD UP TO IT. BUT WHAT CAN I DO? I'M JUST A KID.

WHAM!

I DECIDED TO HEAD FOR THE WOODS AND TRY TO GET IT OFF MY MIND.

THOSE WOODS. SOMETHING FUNNY ABOUT THEM.

WELL, THAT'S WHAT MY WOODS WERE.

D'JA EVER NOTICE, SOMETIMES RIGHT IN THE MIDDLE OF A BIG POPULATED SECTION, THEY GOT A LITTLE STAND OF WOODS, REAL DEEP AND SHADOWY, YOU CAN'T SEE TOO FAR INTO THEM?

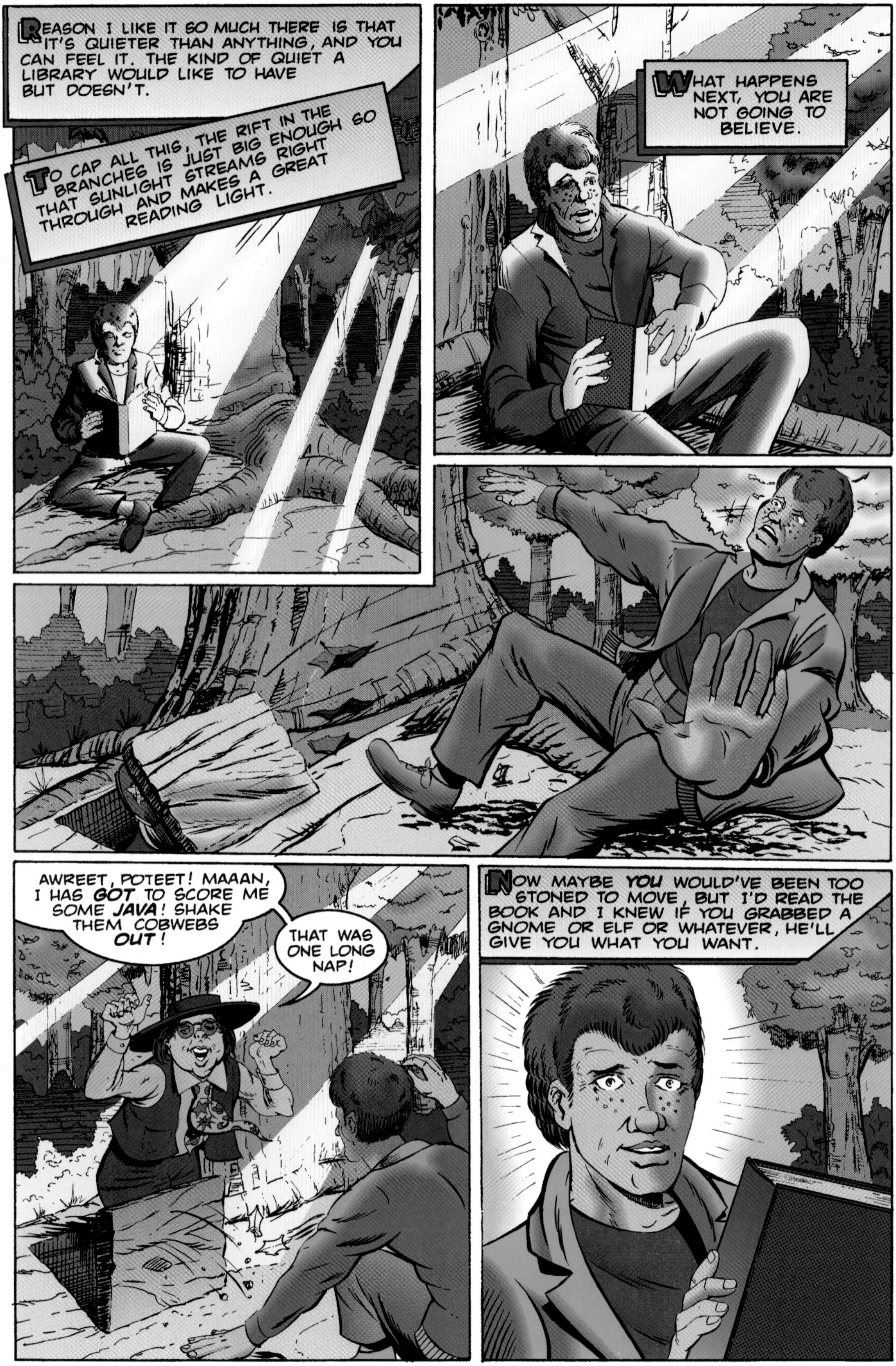

REASON I LIKE IT SO MUCH THERE IS THAT IT'S QUIETER THAN ANYTHING, AND YOU CAN FEEL IT. THE KIND OF QUIET A LIBRARY WOULD LIKE TO HAVE BUT DOESN'T.
TO CAP ALL THIS, THE RIFT IN THE BRANCHES IS JUST BIG ENOUGH SO THAT SUNLIGHT STREAMS RIGHT THROUGH AND MAKES A GREAT READING LIGHT.
WHAT HAPPENS NEXT, YOU ARE NOT GOING TO BELIEVE.
AWREET, POTEET! MAAAN, I HAS **GOT** TO SCORE ME SOME **JAVA**! SHAKE THEM COBWEBS **OUT**!
THAT WAS ONE LONG NAP!
NOW MAYBE **YOU** WOULD'VE BEEN TOO STONED TO MOVE, BUT I'D READ THE BOOK AND I KNEW IF YOU GRABBED A GNOME OR ELF OR WHATEVER, HE'LL GIVE YOU WHAT YOU WANT.

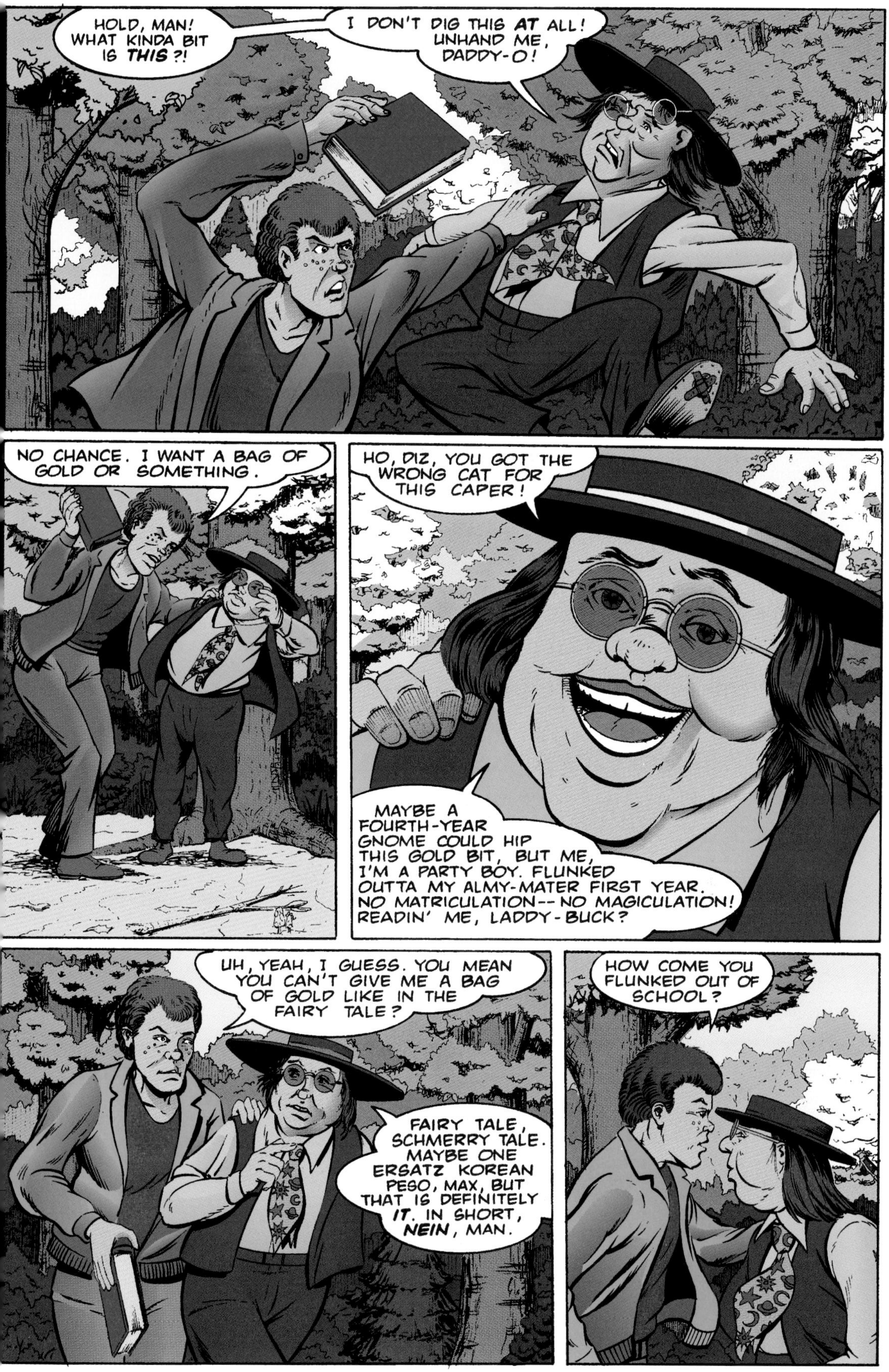
HOLD, MAN! WHAT KINDA BIT IS THIS?!
I DON'T DIG THIS AT ALL! UNHAND ME, DADDY-O!
NO CHANCE. I WANT A BAG OF GOLD OR SOMETHING.
HO, DIZ, YOU GOT THE WRONG CAT FOR THIS CAPER!
MAYBE A FOURTH-YEAR GNOME COULD HIP THIS GOLD BIT, BUT ME, I'M A PARTY BOY. FLUNKED OUTTA MY ALMY-MATER FIRST YEAR. NO MATRICULATION-- NO MAGICULATION! READIN' ME, LADDY-BUCK?
UH, YEAH, I GUESS. YOU MEAN YOU CAN'T GIVE ME A BAG OF GOLD LIKE IN THE FAIRY TALE?
FAIRY TALE, SCHMERRY TALE. MAYBE ONE ERSATZ KOREAN PESO, MAX, BUT THAT IS DEFINITELY IT. IN SHORT, NEIN, MAN.
HOW COME YOU FLUNKED OUT OF SCHOOL?

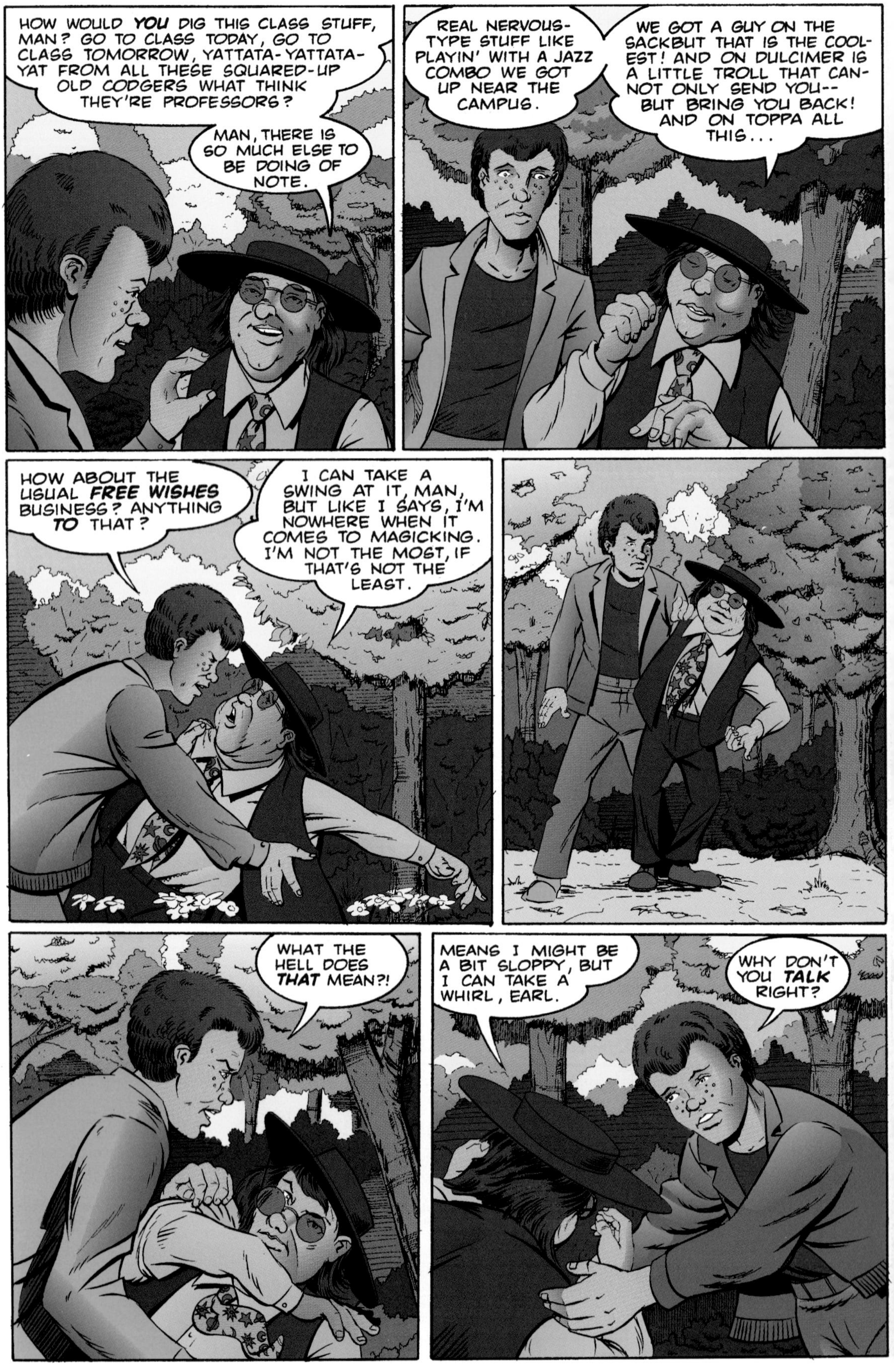
HOW WOULD **YOU** DIG THIS CLASS STUFF, MAN? GO TO CLASS TODAY, GO TO CLASS TOMORROW, YATTATA-YATTATA-YAT FROM ALL THESE SQUARED-UP OLD CODGERS WHAT THINK THEY'RE PROFESSORS?
MAN, THERE IS SO MUCH ELSE TO BE DOING OF NOTE.
REAL NERVOUS-TYPE STUFF LIKE PLAYIN' WITH A JAZZ COMBO WE GOT UP NEAR THE CAMPUS.
WE GOT A GUY ON THE SACKBUT THAT IS THE COOLEST! AND ON DULCIMER IS A LITTLE TROLL THAT CANNOT ONLY SEND YOU-- BUT BRING YOU BACK! AND ON TOPPA ALL THIS...
HOW ABOUT THE USUAL **FREE WISHES** BUSINESS? ANYTHING **TO** THAT?
I CAN TAKE A SWING AT IT, MAN, BUT LIKE I SAYS, I'M NOWHERE WHEN IT COMES TO MAGICKING. I'M NOT THE MOST, IF THAT'S NOT THE LEAST.
WHAT THE HELL DOES **THAT** MEAN?!
MEANS I MIGHT BE A BIT SLOPPY, BUT I CAN TAKE A WHIRL, EARL.
WHY DON'T YOU **TALK** RIGHT?

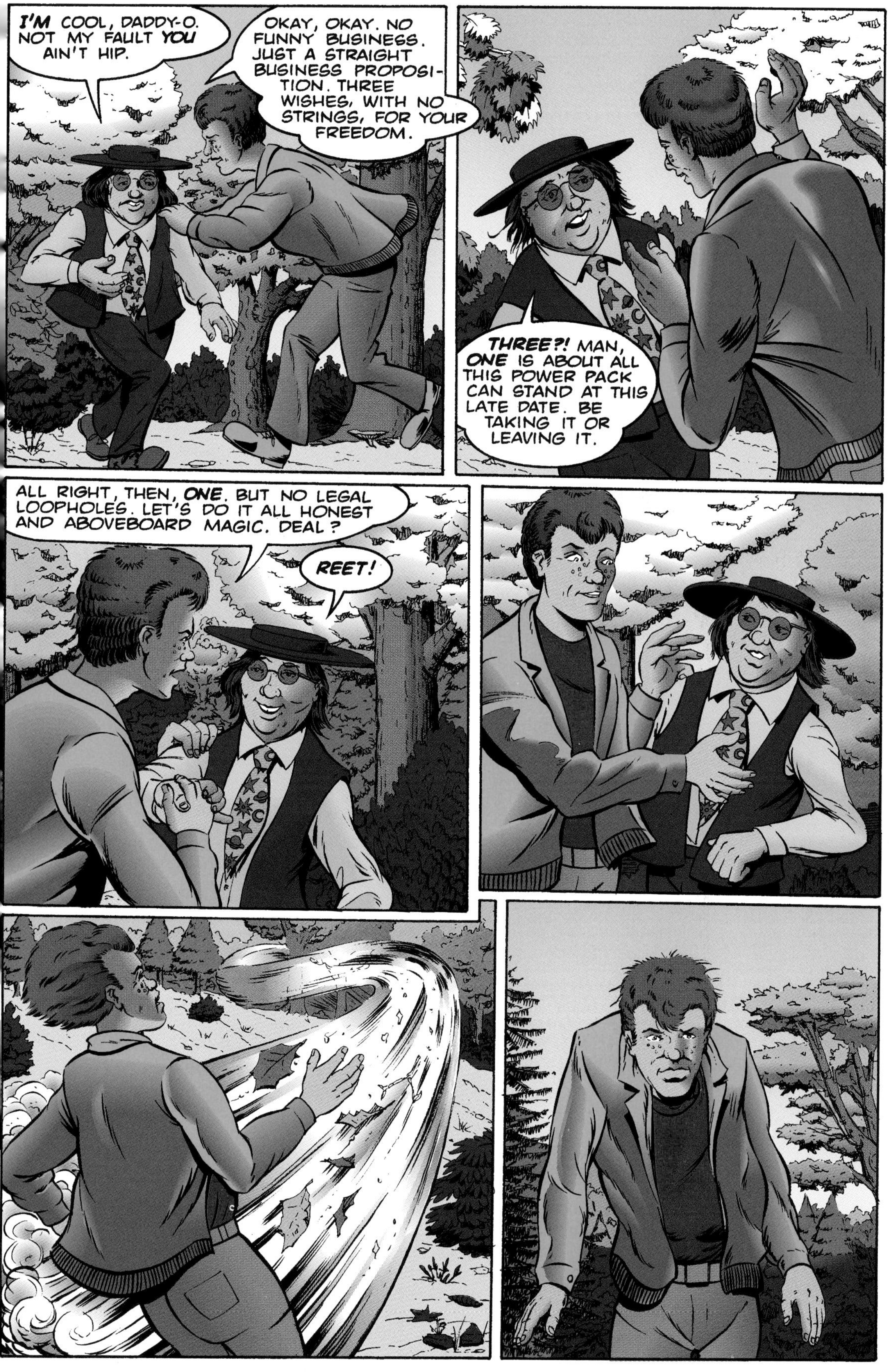
I'M COOL, DADDY-O. NOT MY FAULT YOU AIN'T HIP.
OKAY, OKAY. NO FUNNY BUSINESS. JUST A STRAIGHT BUSINESS PROPOSI-TION. THREE WISHES, WITH NO STRINGS, FOR YOUR FREEDOM.
THREE?! MAN, ONE IS ABOUT ALL THIS POWER PACK CAN STAND AT THIS LATE DATE. BE TAKING IT OR LEAVING IT.
ALL RIGHT, THEN, ONE. BUT NO LEGAL LOOPHOLES. LET'S DO IT ALL HONEST AND ABOVEBOARD MAGIC. DEAL?
REET!

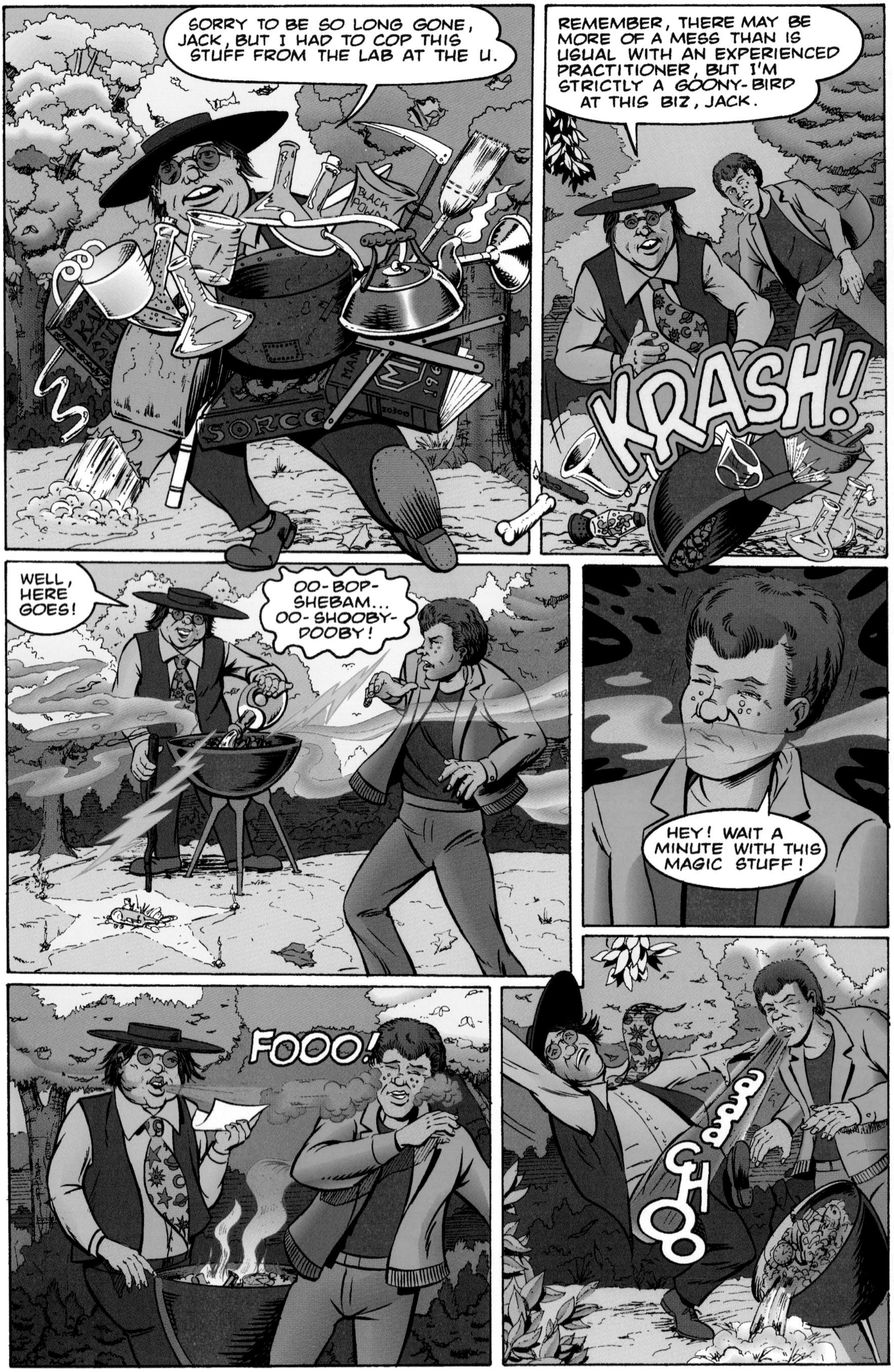
SORRY TO BE SO LONG GONE, JACK, BUT I HAD TO COP THIS STUFF FROM THE LAB AT THE U.
REMEMBER, THERE MAY BE MORE OF A MESS THAN IS USUAL WITH AN EXPERIENCED PRACTITIONER, BUT I'M STRICTLY A GOONY-BIRD AT THIS BIZ, JACK.
KRASH!
WELL, HERE GOES!
OO-BOP-SHEBAM... OO-SHOOBY-DOOBY!
HEY! WAIT A MINUTE WITH THIS MAGIC STUFF!
FOOO!

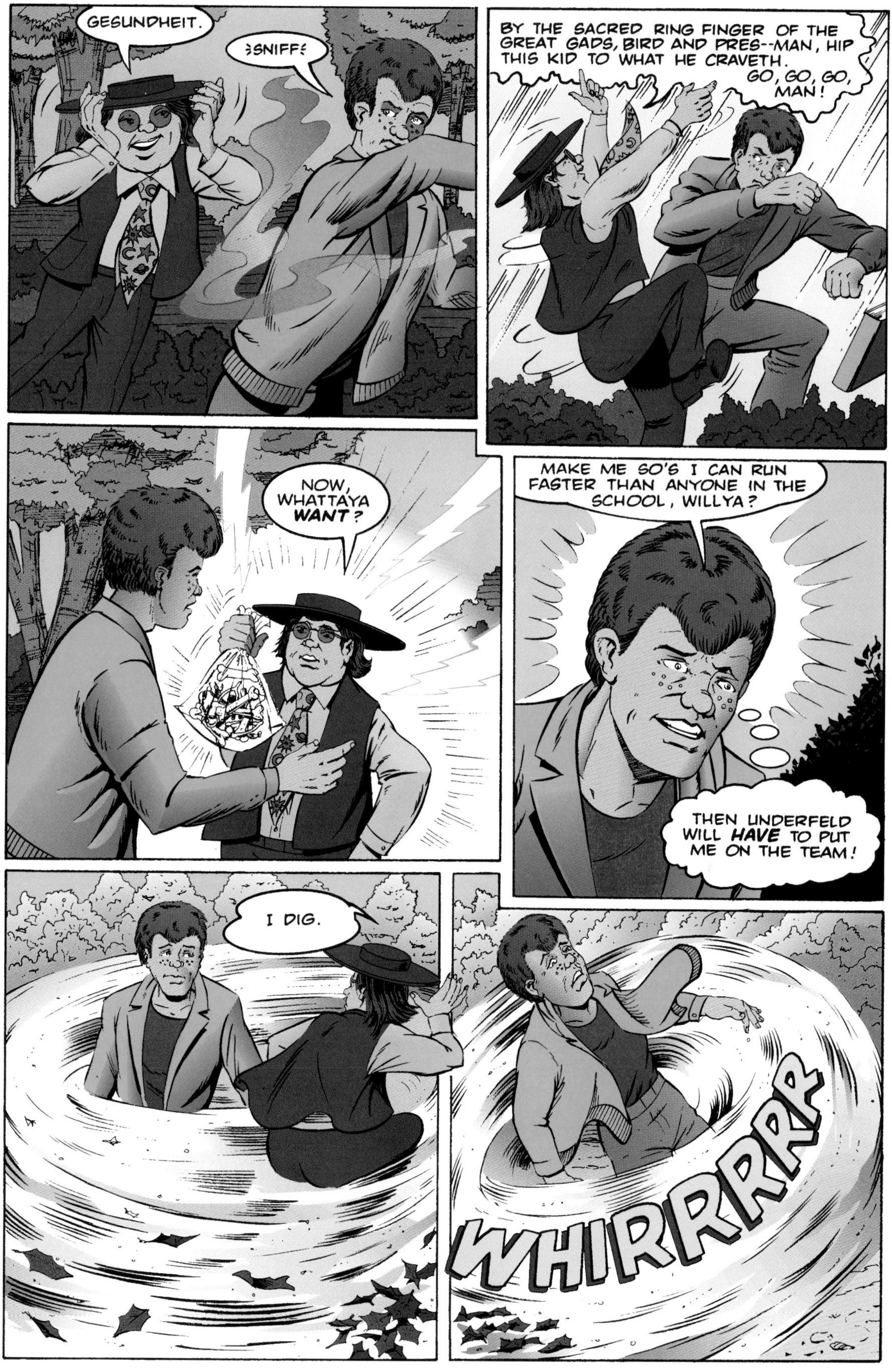
GESUNDHEIT.
SNIFF
BY THE SACRED RING FINGER OF THE GREAT GADS, BIRD AND PRES--MAN, HIP THIS KID TO WHAT HE CRAVETH.
GO, GO, GO, MAN!
NOW, WHATTAYA WANT?
MAKE ME SO'S I CAN RUN FASTER THAN ANYONE IN THE SCHOOL, WILLYA?
THEN UNDERFELD WILL HAVE TO PUT ME ON THE TEAM!
I DIG.
WHIRRRRR

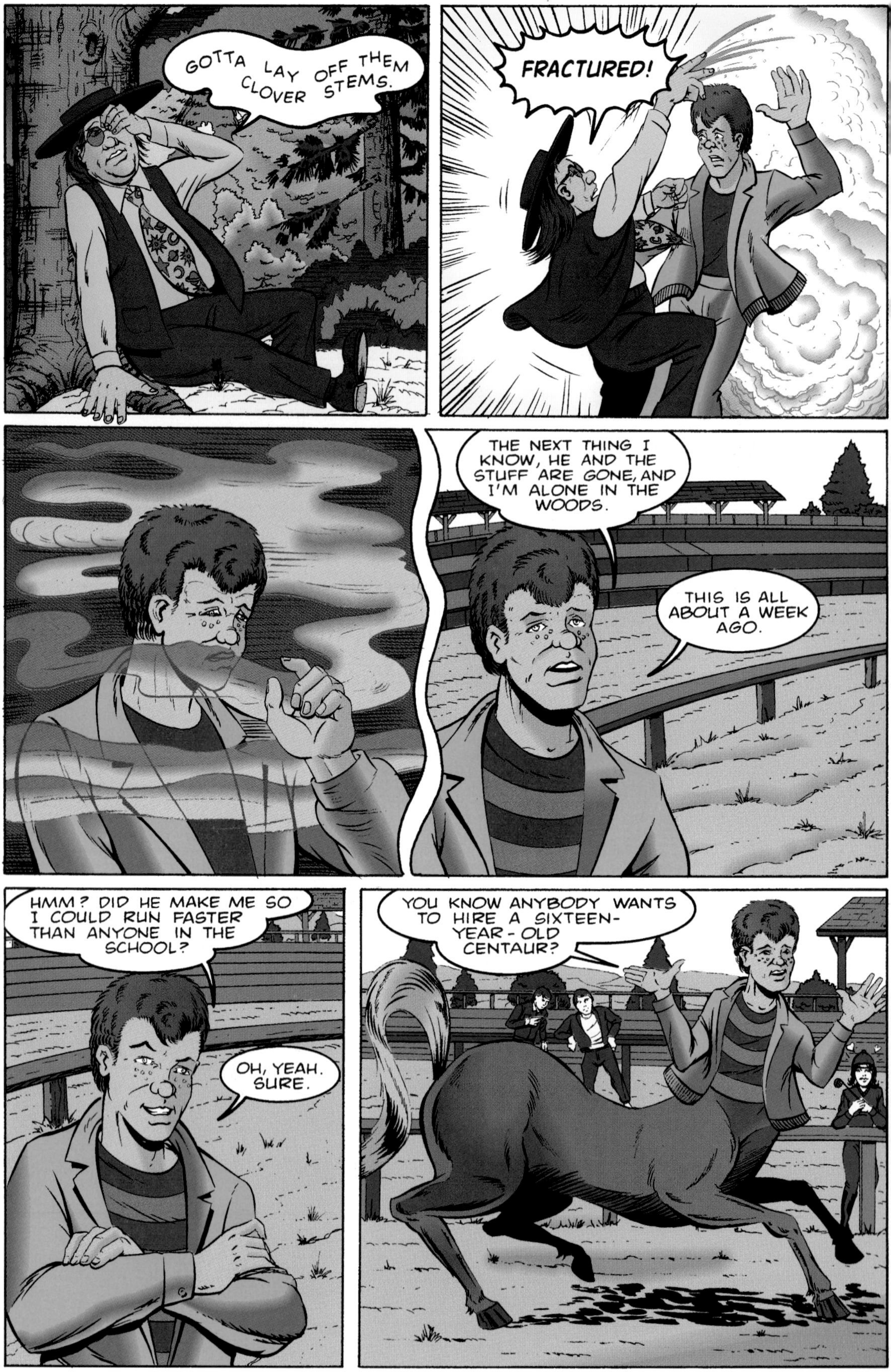
GOTTA LAY OFF THEM CLOVER STEMS.
FRACTURED!
THE NEXT THING I KNOW, HE AND THE STUFF ARE GONE, AND I'M ALONE IN THE WOODS.
THIS IS ALL ABOUT A WEEK AGO.
HMM? DID HE MAKE ME SO I COULD RUN FASTER THAN ANYONE IN THE SCHOOL?
OH, YEAH. SURE.
YOU KNOW ANYBODY WANTS TO HIRE A SIXTEEN-YEAR-OLD CENTAUR?

END!

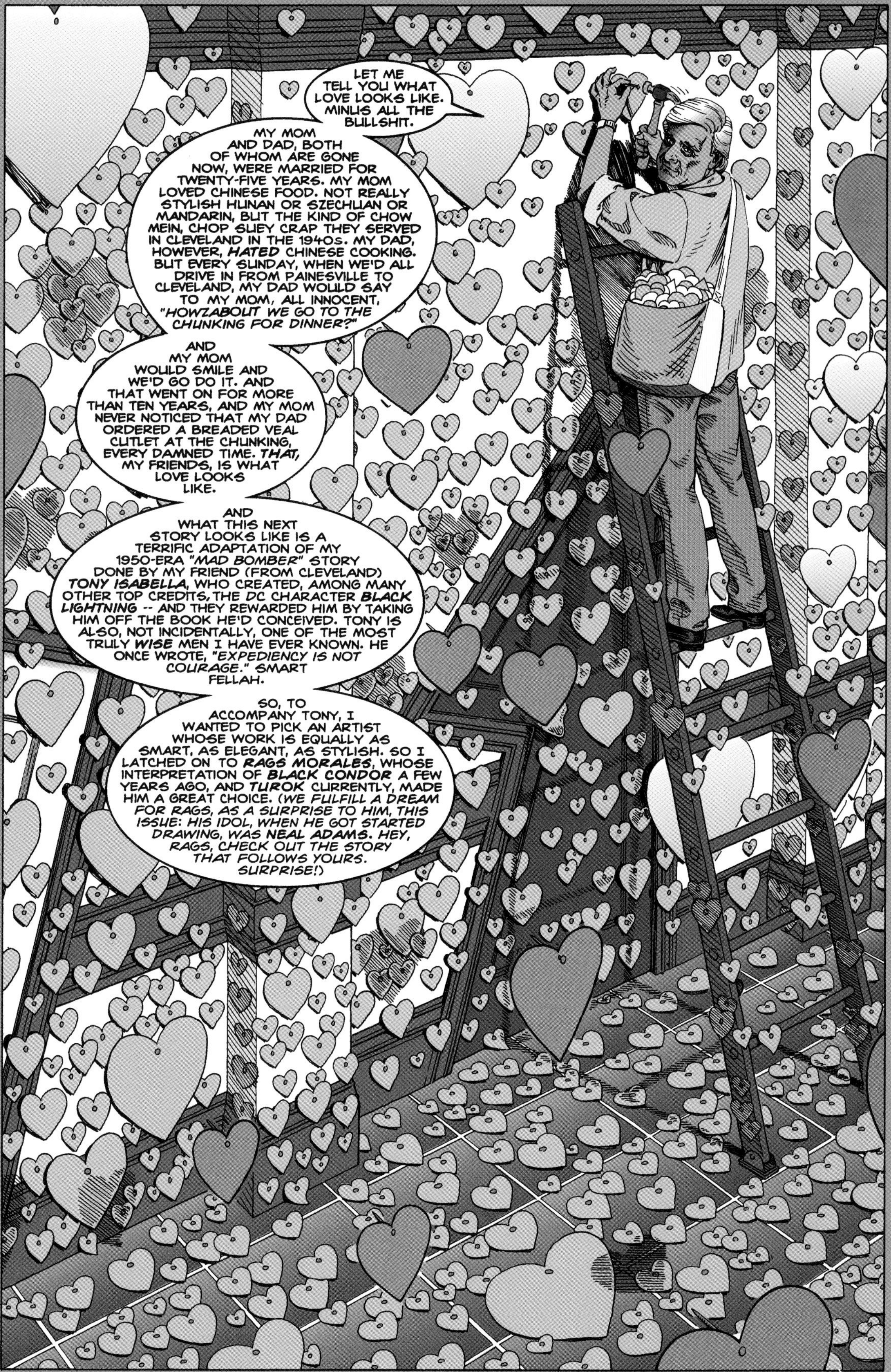
LET ME TELL YOU WHAT LOVE LOOKS LIKE. MINUS ALL THE BULLSHIT.
MY MOM AND DAD, BOTH OF WHOM ARE GONE NOW, WERE MARRIED FOR TWENTY-FIVE YEARS. MY MOM LOVED CHINESE FOOD. NOT REALLY STYLISH HUNAN OR SZECHUAN OR MANDARIN, BUT THE KIND OF CHOW MEIN, CHOP SUEY CRAP THEY SERVED IN CLEVELAND IN THE 1940s. MY DAD, HOWEVER, HATED CHINESE COOKING. BUT EVERY SUNDAY, WHEN WE'D ALL DRIVE IN FROM PAINESVILLE TO CLEVELAND, MY DAD WOULD SAY TO MY MOM, ALL INNOCENT, "HOWZABOUT WE GO TO THE CHUNKING FOR DINNER?"
AND MY MOM WOULD SMILE AND WE'D GO DO IT. AND THAT WENT ON FOR MORE THAN TEN YEARS, AND MY MOM NEVER NOTICED THAT MY DAD ORDERED A BREADED VEAL CUTLET AT THE CHUNKING, EVERY DAMNED TIME. THAT, MY FRIENDS, IS WHAT LOVE LOOKS LIKE.
AND WHAT THIS NEXT STORY LOOKS LIKE IS A TERRIFIC ADAPTATION OF MY 1950-ERA "MAD BOMBER" STORY DONE BY MY FRIEND (FROM CLEVELAND) TONY ISABELLA, WHO CREATED, AMONG MANY OTHER TOP CREDITS, THE DC CHARACTER BLACK LIGHTNING -- AND THEY REWARDED HIM BY TAKING HIM OFF THE BOOK HE'D CONCEIVED. TONY IS ALSO, NOT INCIDENTALLY, ONE OF THE MOST TRULY WISE MEN I HAVE EVER KNOWN. HE ONCE WROTE, "EXPEDIENCY IS NOT COURAGE." SMART FELLAH.
SO, TO ACCOMPANY TONY, I WANTED TO PICK AN ARTIST WHOSE WORK IS EQUALLY AS SMART, AS ELEGANT, AS STYLISH. SO I LATCHED ON TO RAGS MORALES, WHOSE INTERPRETATION OF BLACK CONDOR A FEW YEARS AGO, AND TUROK CURRENTLY, MADE HIM A GREAT CHOICE. (WE FULFILL A DREAM FOR RAGS, AS A SURPRISE TO HIM, THIS ISSUE: HIS IDOL, WHEN HE GOT STARTED DRAWING, WAS NEAL ADAMS. HEY, RAGS, CHECK OUT THE STORY THAT FOLLOWS YOURS. SURPRISE!)

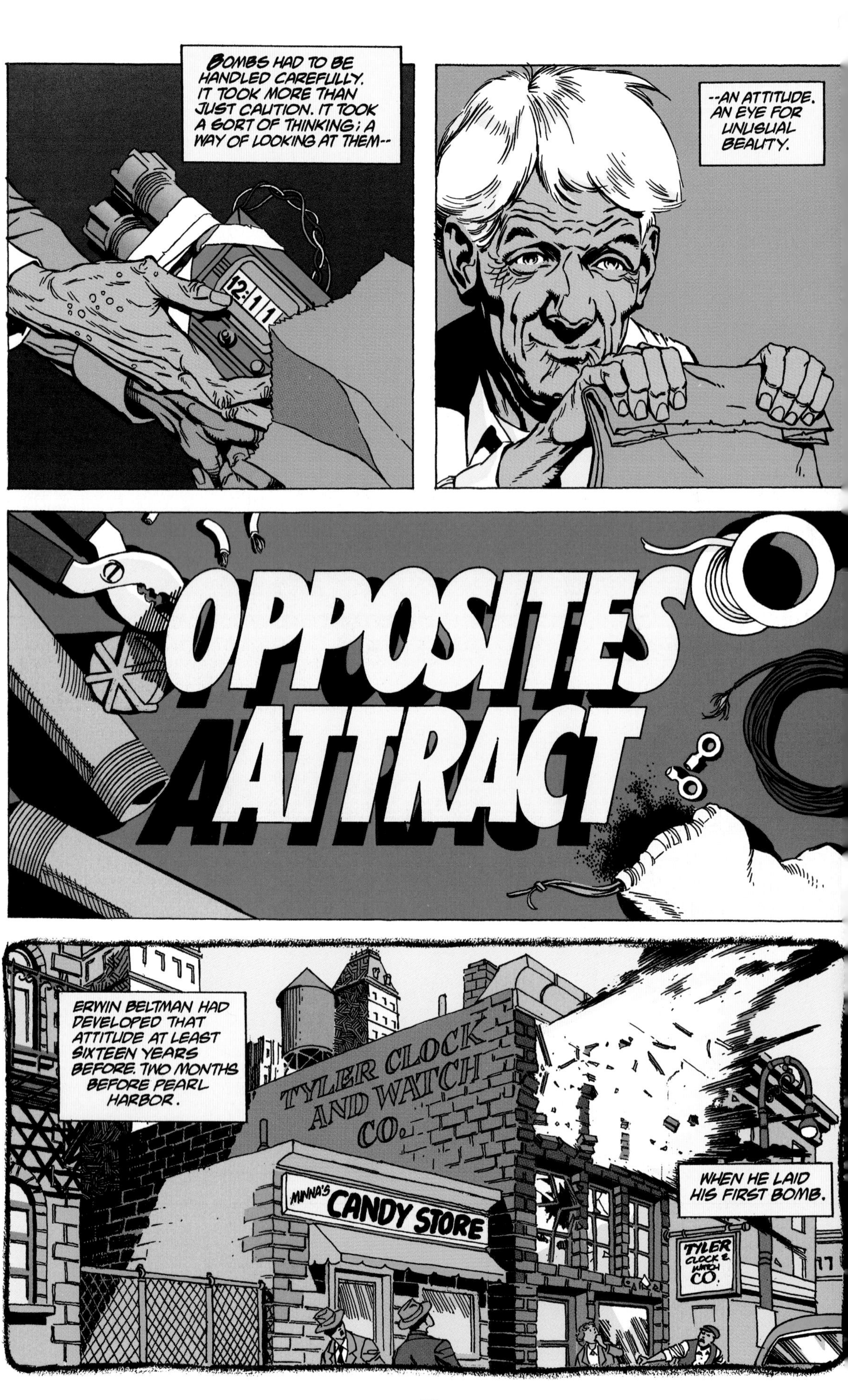
BOMBS HAD TO BE HANDLED CAREFULLY. IT TOOK MORE THAN JUST CAUTION. IT TOOK A SORT OF THINKING; A WAY OF LOOKING AT THEM--
12:11
--AN ATTITUDE. AN EYE FOR UNUSUAL BEAUTY.
OPPOSITES ATTRACT
ERWIN BELTMAN HAD DEVELOPED THAT ATTITUDE AT LEAST SIXTEEN YEARS BEFORE. TWO MONTHS BEFORE PEARL HARBOR.
TYLER CLOCK AND WATCH CO.
MINNA'S CANDY STORE
TYLER CLOCK & WATCH CO.
WHEN HE LAID HIS FIRST BOMB.

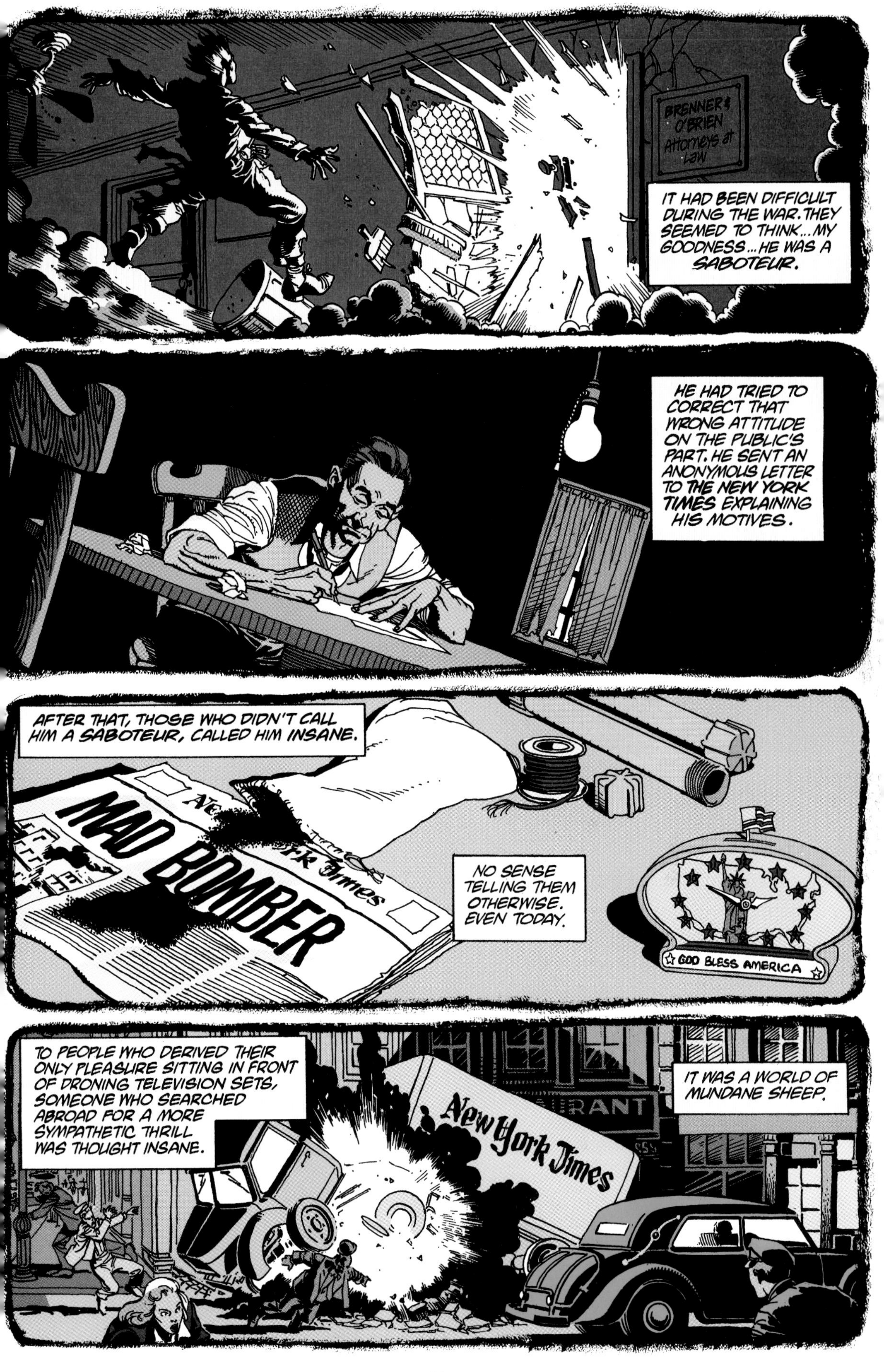
BRENNER & O'BRIEN Attorneys at Law
IT HAD BEEN DIFFICULT DURING THE WAR. THEY SEEMED TO THINK... MY GOODNESS... HE WAS A SABOTEUR.
HE HAD TRIED TO CORRECT THAT WRONG ATTITUDE ON THE PUBLIC'S PART. HE SENT AN ANONYMOUS LETTER TO THE NEW YORK TIMES EXPLAINING HIS MOTIVES.
AFTER THAT, THOSE WHO DIDN'T CALL HIM A SABOTEUR, CALLED HIM INSANE.
MAD BOMBER
NO SENSE TELLING THEM OTHERWISE. EVEN TODAY.
GOD BLESS AMERICA
TO PEOPLE WHO DERIVED THEIR ONLY PLEASURE SITTING IN FRONT OF DRONING TELEVISION SETS, SOMEONE WHO SEARCHED ABROAD FOR A MORE SYMPATHETIC THRILL WAS THOUGHT INSANE.
New York Times
IT WAS A WORLD OF MUNDANE SHEEP.

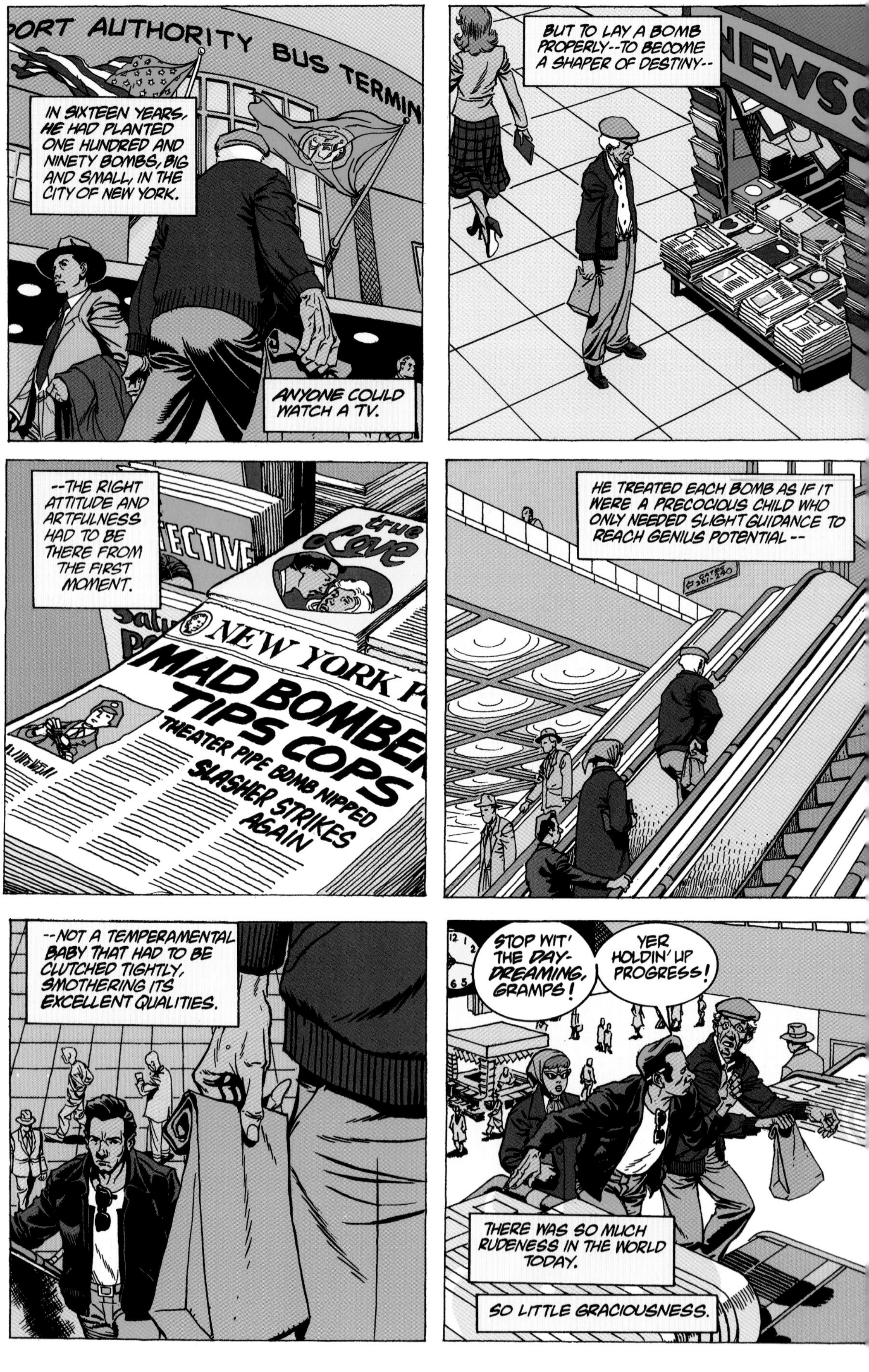

AUTHORITY BUS
IN SIXTEEN YEARS, HE HAD PLANTED ONE HUNDRED AND NINETY BOMBS, BIG AND SMALL, IN THE CITY OF NEW YORK.
ANYONE COULD WATCH A TV.
BUT TO LAY A BOMB PROPERLY--TO BECOME A SHAPER OF DESTINY--
--THE RIGHT ATTITUDE AND ARTFULNESS HAD TO BE THERE FROM THE FIRST MOMENT.
true Love
NEW YORK
MAD BOMBER TIPS COPS
THEATER PIPE BOMB NIPPED
SLASHER STRIKES AGAIN
HE TREATED EACH BOMB AS IF IT WERE A PRECOCIOUS CHILD WHO ONLY NEEDED SLIGHT GUIDANCE TO REACH GENIUS POTENTIAL--
--NOT A TEMPERAMENTAL BABY THAT HAD TO BE CLUTCHED TIGHTLY, SMOTHERING ITS EXCELLENT QUALITIES.
STOP WIT' THE DAY-DREAMING, GRAMPS!
YER HOLDIN' UP PROGRESS!
THERE WAS SO MUCH RUDENESS IN THE WORLD TODAY.
SO LITTLE GRACIOUSNESS.

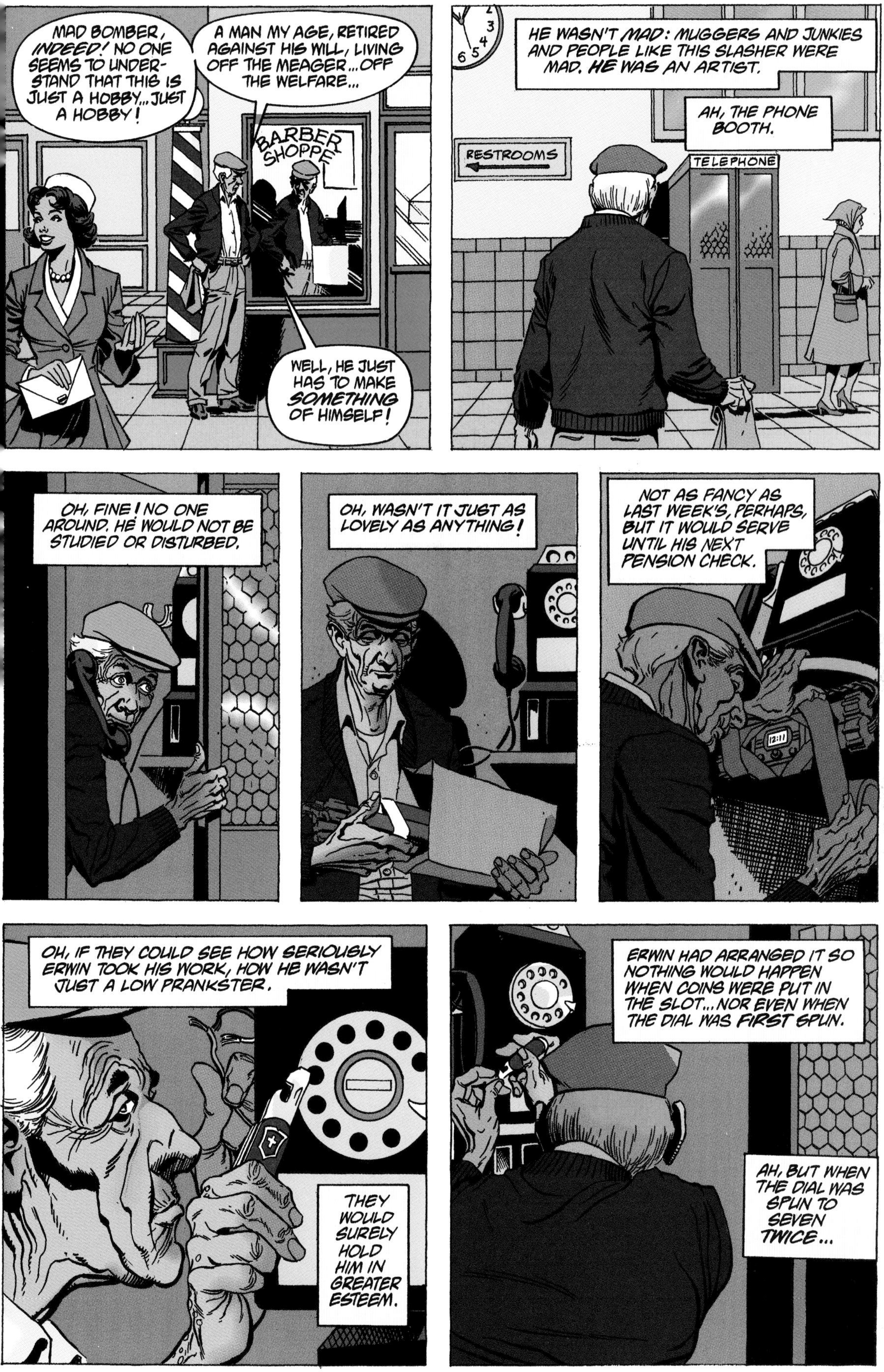
MAD BOMBER, INDEED! NO ONE SEEMS TO UNDERSTAND THAT THIS IS JUST A HOBBY... JUST A HOBBY!
A MAN MY AGE, RETIRED AGAINST HIS WILL, LIVING OFF THE MEAGER... OFF THE WELFARE...
BARBER SHOPPE
WELL, HE JUST HAS TO MAKE SOMETHING OF HIMSELF!
HE WASN'T MAD: MUGGERS AND JUNKIES AND PEOPLE LIKE THIS SLASHER WERE MAD. HE WAS AN ARTIST.
AH, THE PHONE BOOTH.
RESTROOMS
TELEPHONE
OH, FINE! NO ONE AROUND. HE WOULD NOT BE STUDIED OR DISTURBED.
OH, WASN'T IT JUST AS LOVELY AS ANYTHING!
NOT AS FANCY AS LAST WEEK'S, PERHAPS, BUT IT WOULD SERVE UNTIL HIS NEXT PENSION CHECK.
OH, IF THEY COULD SEE HOW SERIOUSLY ERWIN TOOK HIS WORK, HOW HE WASN'T JUST A LOW PRANKSTER.
THEY WOULD SURELY HOLD HIM IN GREATER ESTEEM.
ERWIN HAD ARRANGED IT SO NOTHING WOULD HAPPEN WHEN COINS WERE PUT IN THE SLOT... NOR EVEN WHEN THE DIAL WAS FIRST SPUN.
AH, BUT WHEN THE DIAL WAS SPUN TO SEVEN TWICE...

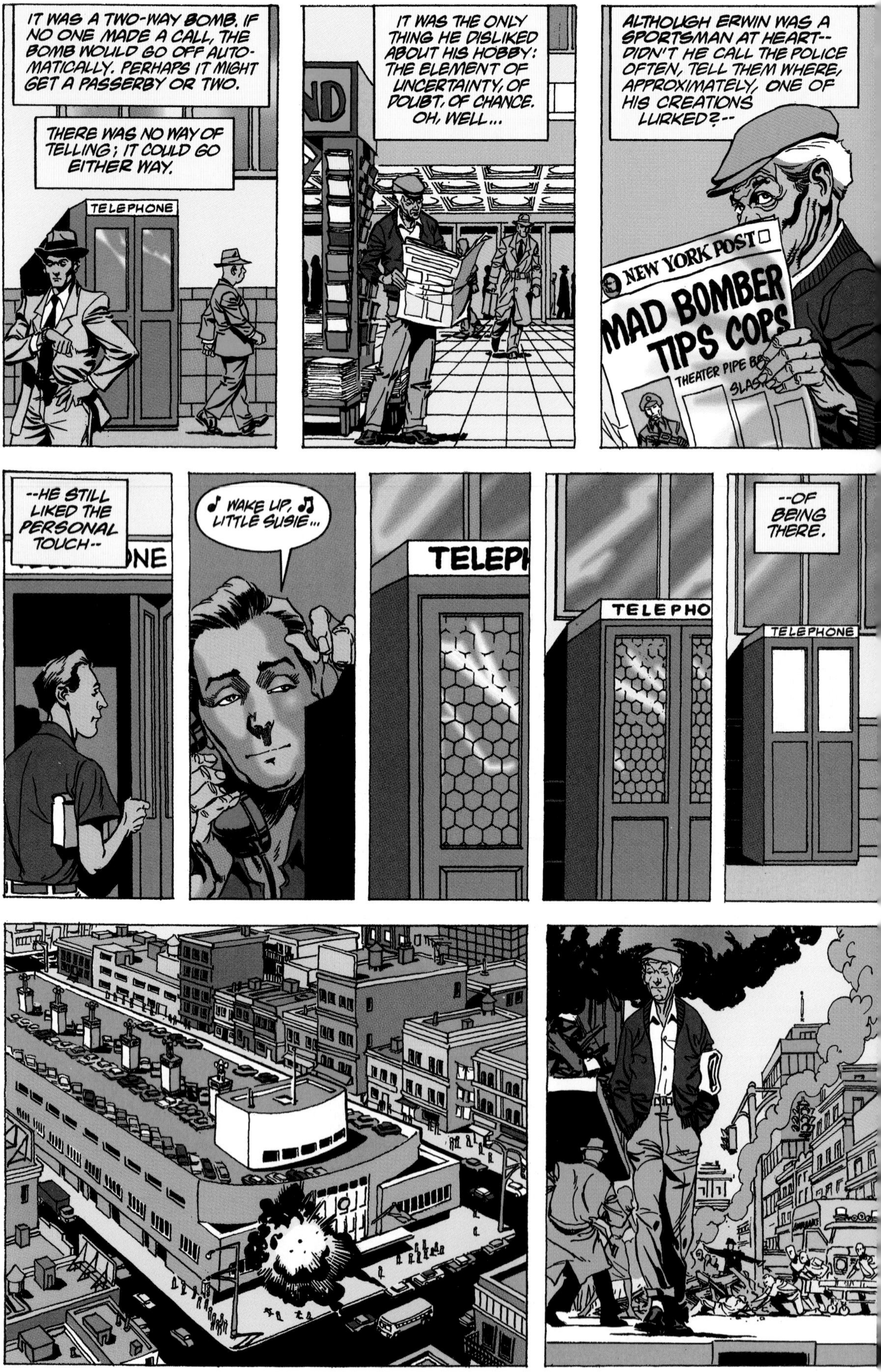
IT WAS A TWO-WAY BOMB. IF NO ONE MADE A CALL, THE BOMB WOULD GO OFF AUTOMATICALLY. PERHAPS IT MIGHT GET A PASSERBY OR TWO.
THERE WAS NO WAY OF TELLING; IT COULD GO EITHER WAY.
TELEPHONE
IT WAS THE ONLY THING HE DISLIKED ABOUT HIS HOBBY: THE ELEMENT OF UNCERTAINTY, OF DOUBT, OF CHANCE. OH, WELL...
ALTHOUGH ERWIN WAS A SPORTSMAN AT HEART-- DIDN'T HE CALL THE POLICE OFTEN, TELL THEM WHERE, APPROXIMATELY, ONE OF HIS CREATIONS LURKED?--
NEW YORK POST
MAD BOMBER TIPS COPS
--HE STILL LIKED THE PERSONAL TOUCH--
♪ WAKE UP, ♫ LITTLE SUSIE...
TELEPH
TELEPHO
TELEPHONE
--OF BEING THERE.

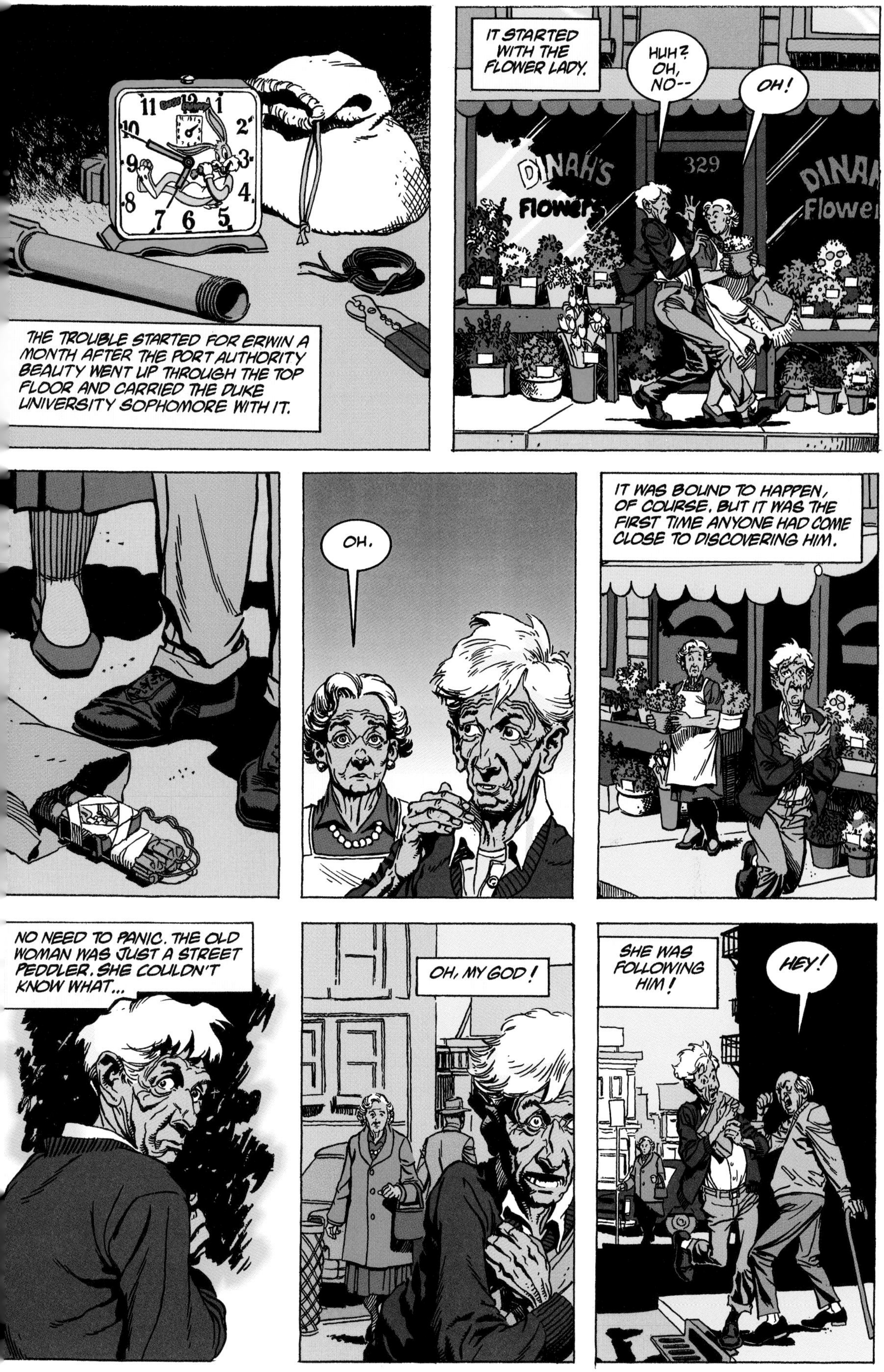

11
12
1
2
3
4
5
6
7
8
9
10
THE TROUBLE STARTED FOR ERWIN A MONTH AFTER THE PORT AUTHORITY BEAUTY WENT UP THROUGH THE TOP FLOOR AND CARRIED THE DUKE UNIVERSITY SOPHOMORE WITH IT.
IT STARTED WITH THE FLOWER LADY.
HUH? OH, NO--
OH!
DINAH'S Flowers
329
OH.
IT WAS BOUND TO HAPPEN, OF COURSE. BUT IT WAS THE FIRST TIME ANYONE HAD COME CLOSE TO DISCOVERING HIM.
NO NEED TO PANIC. THE OLD WOMAN WAS JUST A STREET PEDDLER. SHE COULDN'T KNOW WHAT...
OH, MY GOD!
SHE WAS FOLLOWING HIM!
HEY!

ERWIN WAS FRIGHTENED; HE HAD SEEN HER EIGHT TIMES SINCE THAT TERRIBLE DAY. SHE OBVIOUSLY KNEW WHO HE WAS AND WHERE HE LIVED...HAD FOLLOWED HIM THAT DAY.

EIGHT SEPARATE MORNINGS, WHEN HE LEFT HIS BUILDING TO PICK UP A PAPER, SHE HAD BEEN SOME-WHERE NEARBY IN PLAIN SIGHT, TRYING TO TORMENT HIM.

THE FIRST MORNING, ERWIN SAW HER ACROSS THE STREET AND VERY NEARLY WALKED INTO A LAMPPOST. HE HAD CREPT BACK TO HIS HOME THROUGH A FILTHY BACK ALLEY.

SO IT HAD GONE FOR EIGHT DAYS, UNTIL ERWIN WAS TOO FRIGHTENED TO LEAVE THE SILENT, STOLID ROOM WHERE HE LIVED ALONE IN THE TOO-SILENT, TOO-STOLID LONELINESS OF HIS OLD AGE.

TOO FRIGHTENED EVEN TO TURN ON THE LIGHTS, SO HE SAT IN THE TOO-SOLID DARKNESS.

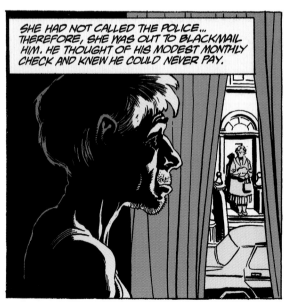

SHE HAD NOT CALLED THE POLICE... THEREFORE, SHE WAS OUT TO BLACKMAIL HIM. HE THOUGHT OF HIS MODEST MONTHLY CHECK AND KNEW HE COULD NEVER PAY.

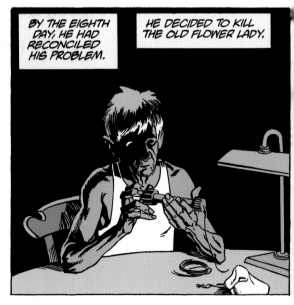

BY THE EIGHTH DAY, HE HAD RECONCILED HIS PROBLEM.

HE DECIDED TO KILL THE OLD FLOWER LADY.

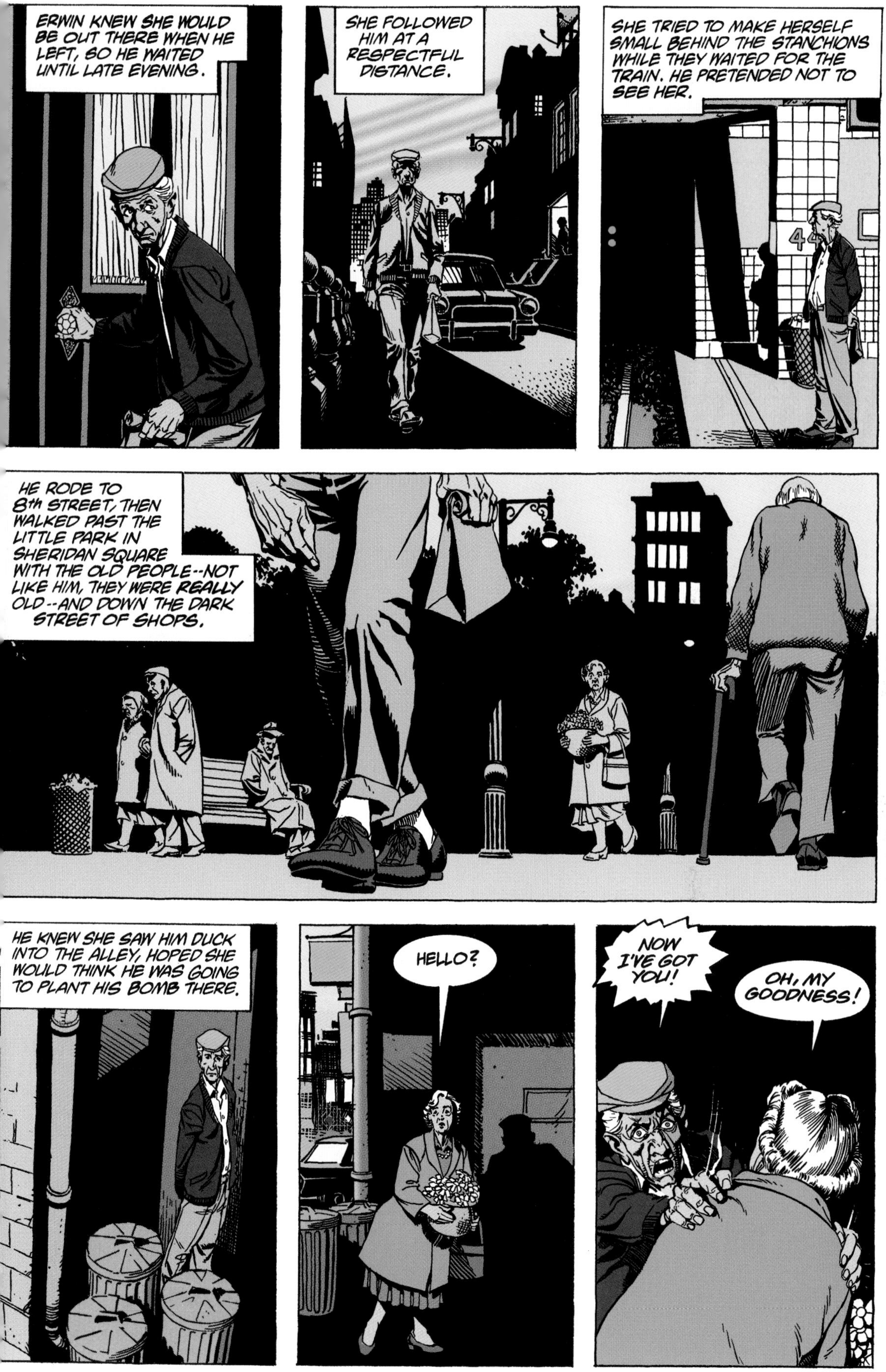
ERWIN KNEW SHE WOULD BE OUT THERE WHEN HE LEFT, SO HE WAITED UNTIL LATE EVENING.
SHE FOLLOWED HIM AT A RESPECTFUL DISTANCE.
SHE TRIED TO MAKE HERSELF SMALL BEHIND THE STANCHIONS WHILE THEY WAITED FOR THE TRAIN. HE PRETENDED NOT TO SEE HER.
HE RODE TO 8th STREET, THEN WALKED PAST THE LITTLE PARK IN SHERIDAN SQUARE WITH THE OLD PEOPLE--NOT LIKE HIM, THEY WERE REALLY OLD--AND DOWN THE DARK STREET OF SHOPS.
HE KNEW SHE SAW HIM DUCK INTO THE ALLEY, HOPED SHE WOULD THINK HE WAS GOING TO PLANT HIS BOMB THERE.
HELLO?
NOW I'VE GOT YOU!
OH, MY GOODNESS!

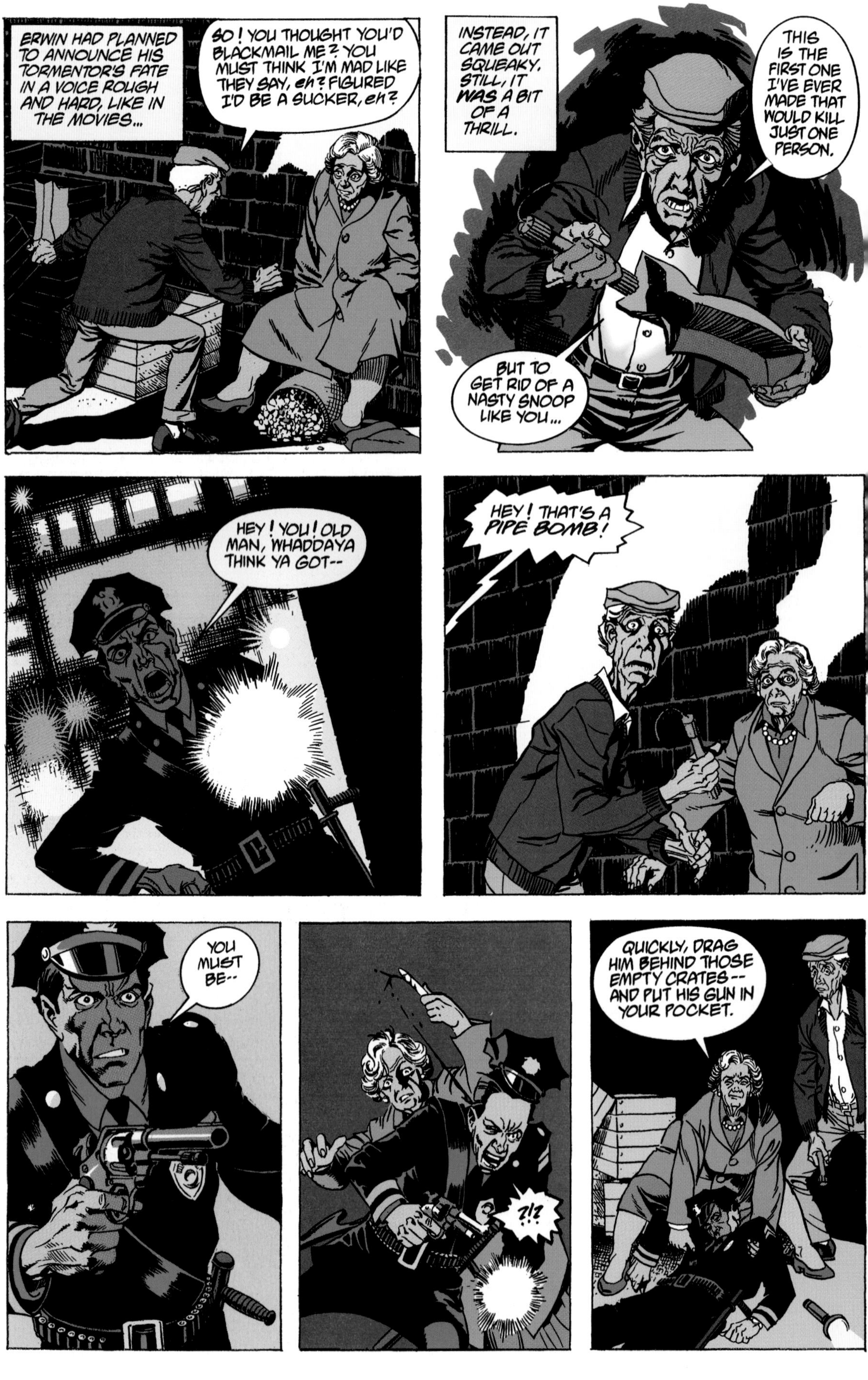
ERWIN HAD PLANNED TO ANNOUNCE HIS TORMENTOR'S FATE IN A VOICE ROUGH AND HARD, LIKE IN THE MOVIES...
SO! YOU THOUGHT YOU'D BLACKMAIL ME? YOU MUST THINK I'M MAD LIKE THEY SAY, eh? FIGURED I'D BE A SUCKER, eh?
INSTEAD, IT CAME OUT SQUEAKY. STILL, IT WAS A BIT OF A THRILL.
THIS IS THE FIRST ONE I'VE EVER MADE THAT WOULD KILL JUST ONE PERSON.
BUT TO GET RID OF A NASTY SNOOP LIKE YOU...
HEY! YOU! OLD MAN, WHADDAYA THINK YA GOT--
HEY! THAT'S A PIPE BOMB!
YOU MUST BE--
?!?
QUICKLY, DRAG HIM BEHIND THOSE EMPTY CRATES-- AND PUT HIS GUN IN YOUR POCKET.

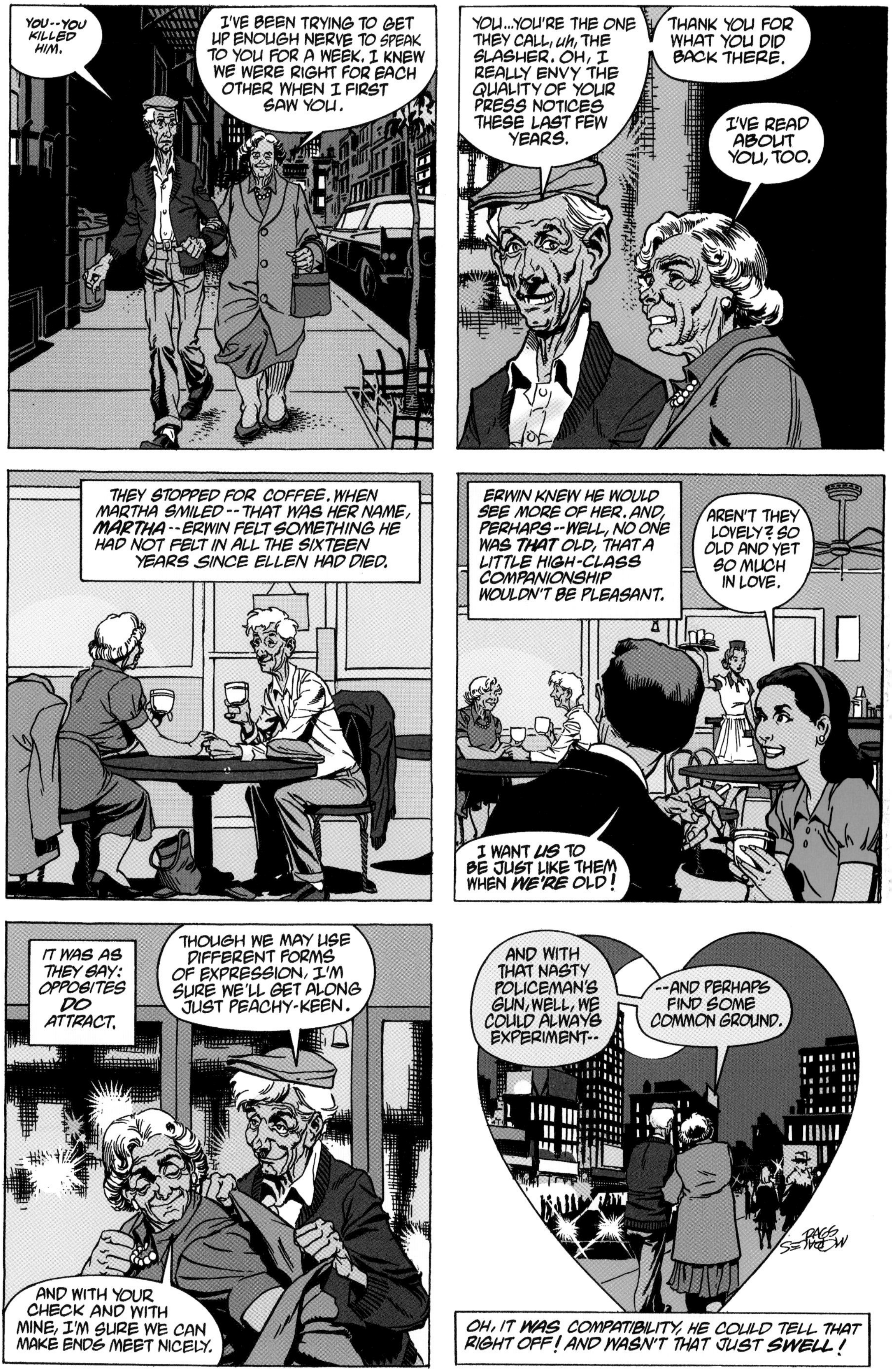
YOU--YOU KILLED HIM.
I'VE BEEN TRYING TO GET UP ENOUGH NERVE TO SPEAK TO YOU FOR A WEEK. I KNEW WE WERE RIGHT FOR EACH OTHER WHEN I FIRST SAW YOU.
YOU...YOU'RE THE ONE THEY CALL, *uh*, THE SLASHER. OH, I REALLY ENVY THE QUALITY OF YOUR PRESS NOTICES THESE LAST FEW YEARS.
THANK YOU FOR WHAT YOU DID BACK THERE.
I'VE READ ABOUT YOU, TOO.
THEY STOPPED FOR COFFEE. WHEN MARTHA SMILED--THAT WAS HER NAME, **MARTHA**--ERWIN FELT **SOMETHING** HE HAD NOT FELT IN ALL THE SIXTEEN YEARS SINCE ELLEN HAD DIED.
ERWIN KNEW HE WOULD SEE MORE OF HER. AND, PERHAPS--WELL, NO ONE WAS **THAT** OLD, THAT A LITTLE HIGH-CLASS COMPANIONSHIP WOULDN'T BE PLEASANT.
AREN'T THEY LOVELY? SO OLD AND YET SO MUCH IN LOVE.
I WANT **US** TO BE JUST LIKE THEM WHEN **WE'RE** OLD!
IT WAS AS THEY SAY: OPPOSITES **DO** ATTRACT.
THOUGH WE MAY USE DIFFERENT FORMS OF EXPRESSION, I'M SURE WE'LL GET ALONG JUST PEACHY-KEEN.
AND WITH YOUR CHECK AND WITH MINE, I'M SURE WE CAN MAKE ENDS MEET NICELY.
AND WITH THAT NASTY POLICEMAN'S GUN, WELL, WE COULD ALWAYS EXPERIMENT--
--AND PERHAPS FIND SOME COMMON GROUND.
OH, IT **WAS** COMPATIBILITY, HE COULD TELL THAT RIGHT OFF! AND WASN'T THAT JUST **SWELL**!

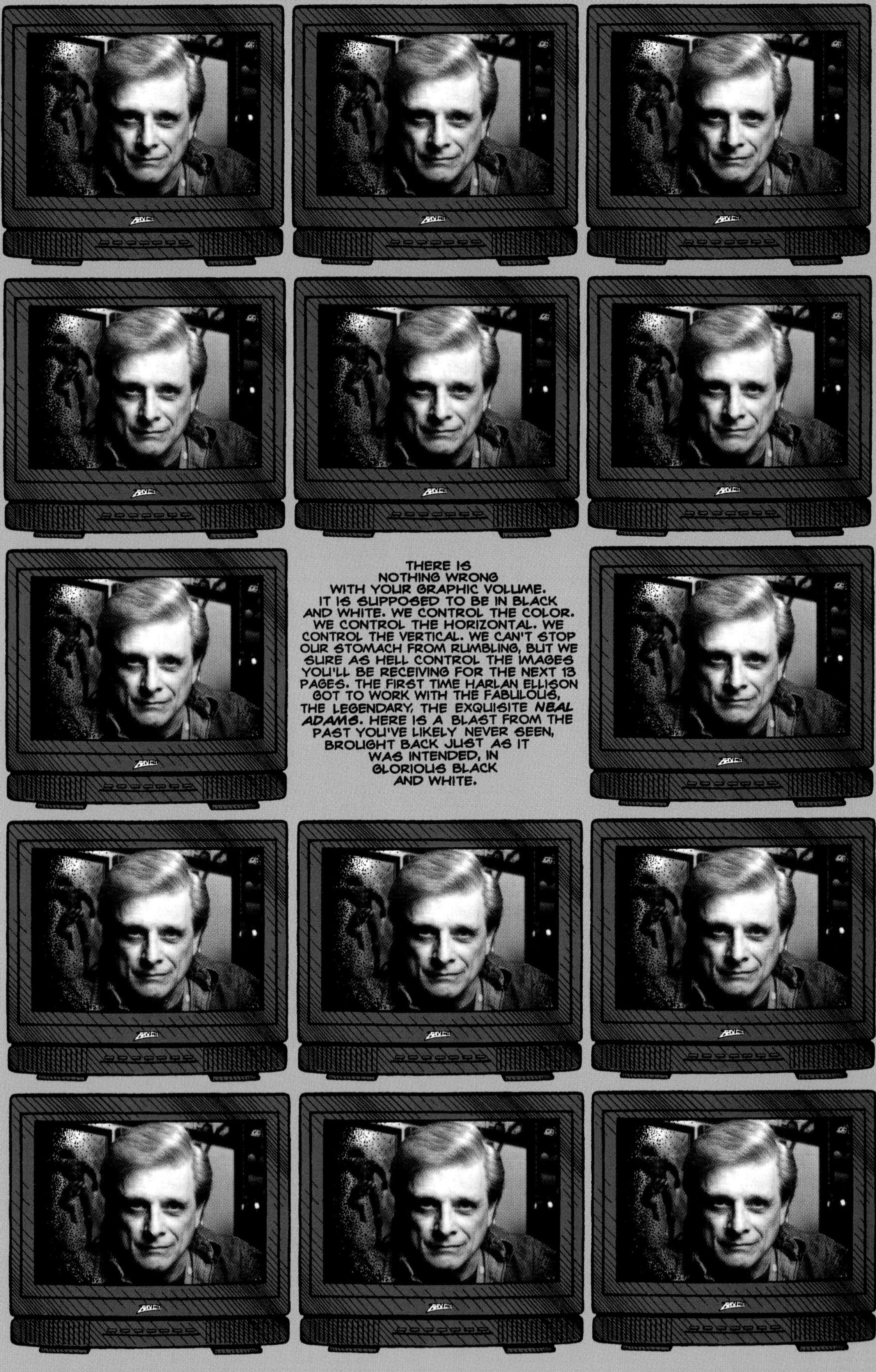
THERE IS NOTHING WRONG WITH YOUR GRAPHIC VOLUME. IT IS SUPPOSED TO BE IN BLACK AND WHITE. WE CONTROL THE COLOR. WE CONTROL THE HORIZONTAL. WE CONTROL THE VERTICAL. WE CAN'T STOP OUR STOMACH FROM RUMBLING, BUT WE SURE AS HELL CONTROL THE IMAGES YOU'LL BE RECEIVING FOR THE NEXT 13 PAGES. THE FIRST TIME HARLAN ELLISON GOT TO WORK WITH THE FABULOUS, THE LEGENDARY, THE EXQUISITE *NEAL ADAMS*. HERE IS A BLAST FROM THE PAST YOU'VE LIKELY NEVER SEEN, BROUGHT BACK JUST AS IT WAS INTENDED, IN GLORIOUS BLACK AND WHITE.

MOIST SHADOW MEN SANG THERE. A STRANGE SONG OF DARK COLORS. TWO PURE-WHITE BULLS WERE BROUGHT, AND RITUAL PURIFICATION WAS ACHIEVED BY CUTTING THEIR THROATS. THEN THE WHITE GOAT, WHOSE BLOOD WAS SIPPED FROM ITS SEVERED, DRIPPING HEART. THEN THE IMMENSE, MANLIKE FIGURES...

...OF TREE LIMBS AND BRANCHES WERE SET ON FIRE, THE BOUND HUMAN SACRIFICES IN THEIR DEPTHS SHRIEKING AS THEY BURNED. THEN THE MOIST SHADOW MEN, WHOM HISTORY WOULD CALL THE LAST BRONZE AGE PEOPLE, THE **WESSEX PEOPLE**, DREW THEIR ANIMAL-HIDE CLOAKS ABOUT THEM,

AND THEY MOVED WITHIN THE CIRCLE OF STANDING CYCLOPEAN STONES AND LINTELS. MOVED WITHIN THE DARK CIRCLE OF STONE-HENGE, AND SWAYED BACK AND FORTH, MURMURING THEIR PRAYERS.

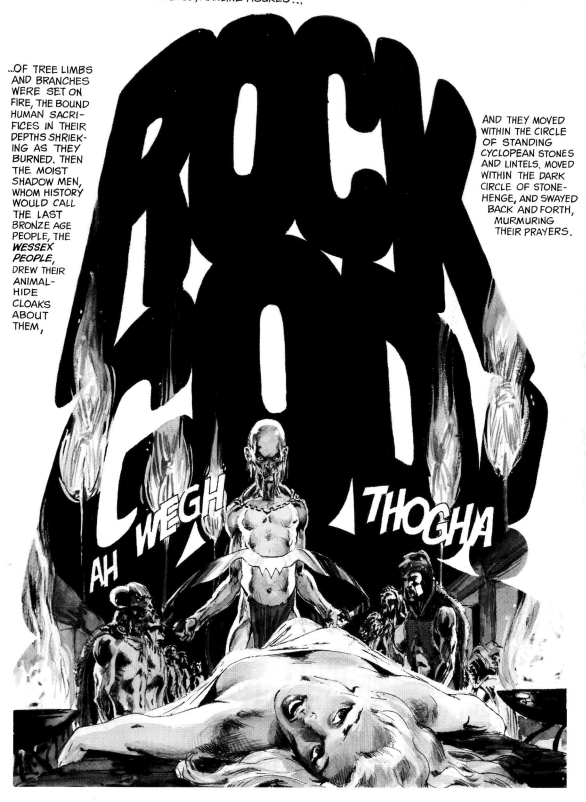

ROCK GOD

AH WEGH ATHOGHA

NAKED, COLD SO COLD IN THE WINTER WIND, THE GREAT PRIEST STOOD ON THE ALTAR STONE, AND HUNG DOWN HIS ARMS AND LET HIS HEAD DROOP FORWARD, AND INVOKED THE LOFTIEST, THE LOWEST PRAYER TO DIS.

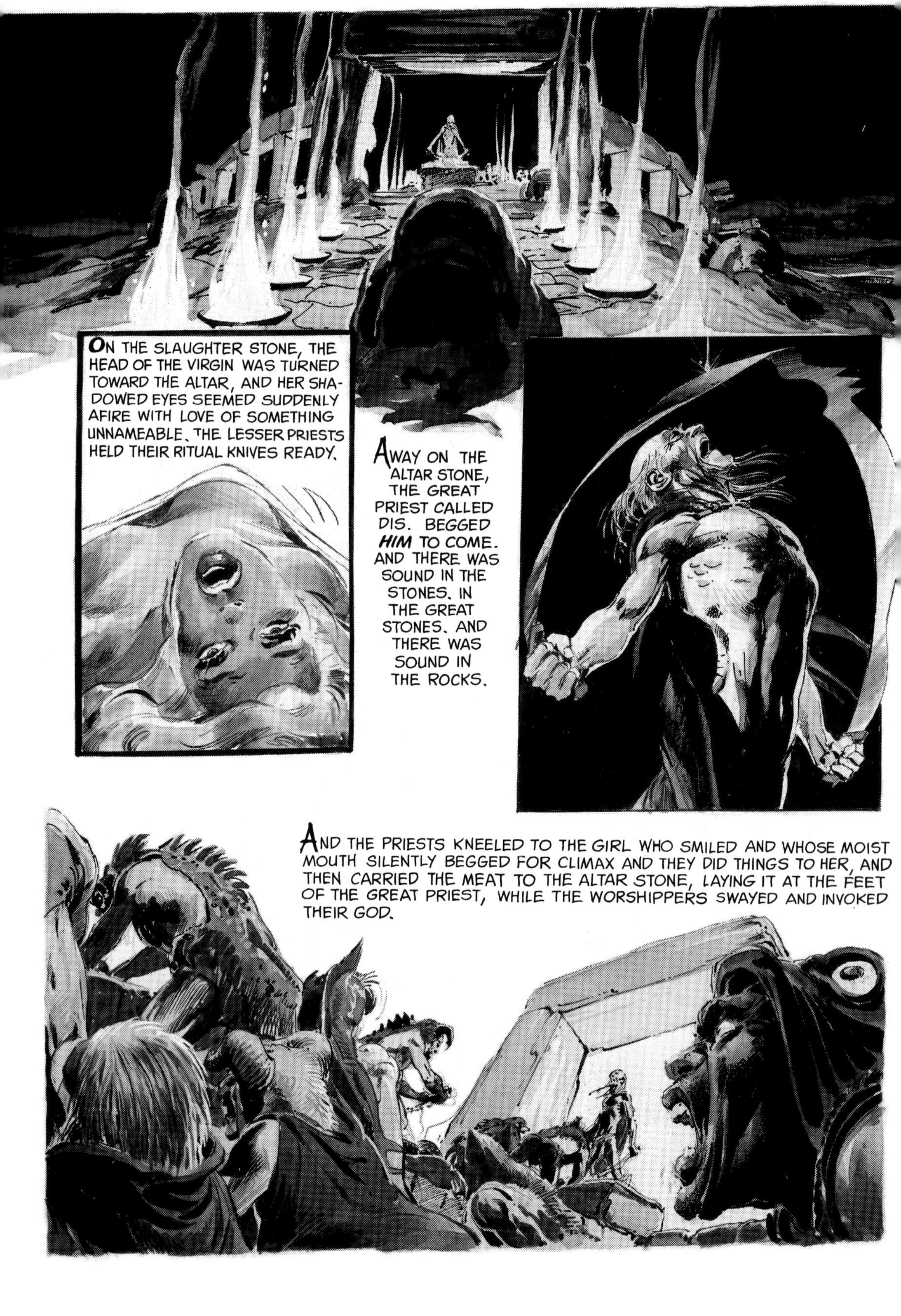

ON THE SLAUGHTER STONE, THE HEAD OF THE VIRGIN WAS TURNED TOWARD THE ALTAR, AND HER SHADOWED EYES SEEMED SUDDENLY AFIRE WITH LOVE OF SOMETHING UNNAMEABLE. THE LESSER PRIESTS HELD THEIR RITUAL KNIVES READY.
AWAY ON THE ALTAR STONE, THE GREAT PRIEST CALLED DIS. BEGGED ***HIM*** TO COME. AND THERE WAS SOUND IN THE STONES. IN THE GREAT STONES. AND THERE WAS SOUND IN THE ROCKS.
AND THE PRIESTS KNEELED TO THE GIRL WHO SMILED AND WHOSE MOIST MOUTH SILENTLY BEGGED FOR CLIMAX AND THEY DID THINGS TO HER, AND THEN CARRIED THE MEAT TO THE ALTAR STONE, LAYING IT AT THE FEET OF THE GREAT PRIEST, WHILE THE WORSHIPPERS SWAYED AND INVOKED THEIR GOD.

DARKNESS FLOWED AS THE SOUNDS OF GREAT HEAVINGS IN THE ROCKS GREW LOUDER. THEN DIS CAME. GREAT, DARK DIS CAME. THEY STARED THROUGH THE MASSIVE ARCHWAY TOWARD THE HEEL STONE. THE FIRST FAINT GLIMMER OF SUNRISE SPLASHED ITS POLISHED DOME. AND THE HEEL STONE BEGAN TO CHANGE.

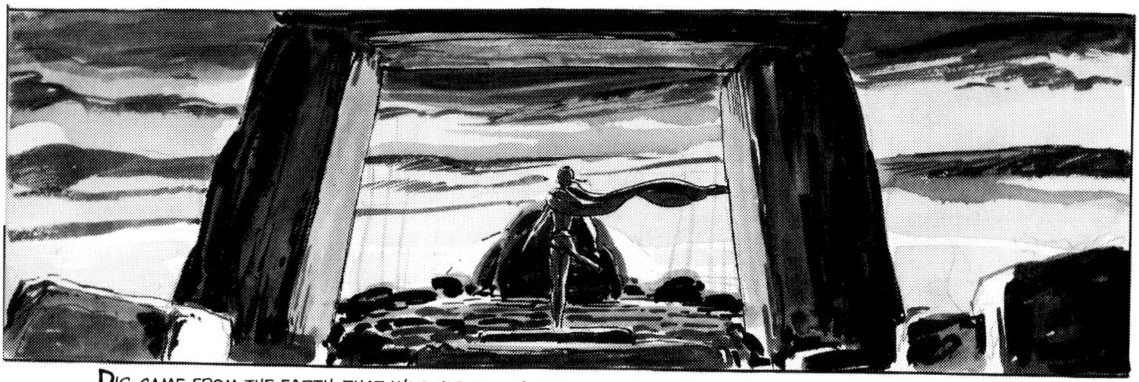

DIS CAME FROM THE EARTH THAT WAS HIS FLESH. THE ROCK THAT WAS HIS BONE. THE STONE THAT WAS HIS HOME, HIS ESSENCE. THE SUNRISE CEASED. NIGHT CAME AGAIN. WASHING UP OUT OF THE EARTH, AND THE WORLD WENT DARK.

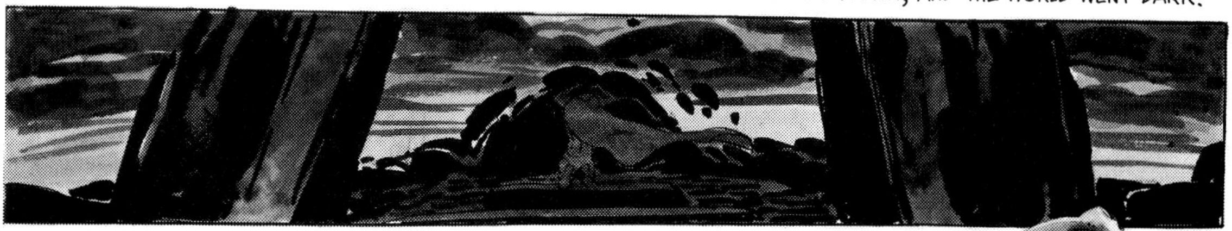

THE HEEL STONE SHIFTED SHAPE AND GREW, AND, RISING FROM THE INANIMATE STONE, DIS TOOK FORM. HAIRLESS FLESH AS SOLID AS MOUNTAINS. TRILOTHONS, SARSEN STONE, SLAUGHTER STONE, LINTELS, BLUE STONE HORSESHOE... FED THE BODY OF DIS WITH THEIR SUBSTANCE, AND HE GREW. MASSIVE, ENORMOUS, RISING INTO THE NIGHT GREATER THAN THE STONES. TWO HUNDRED, THREE HUNDRED FEET, TOWERING OVER THE AWE AND SUPPLICATING WESSEX PEOPLE.

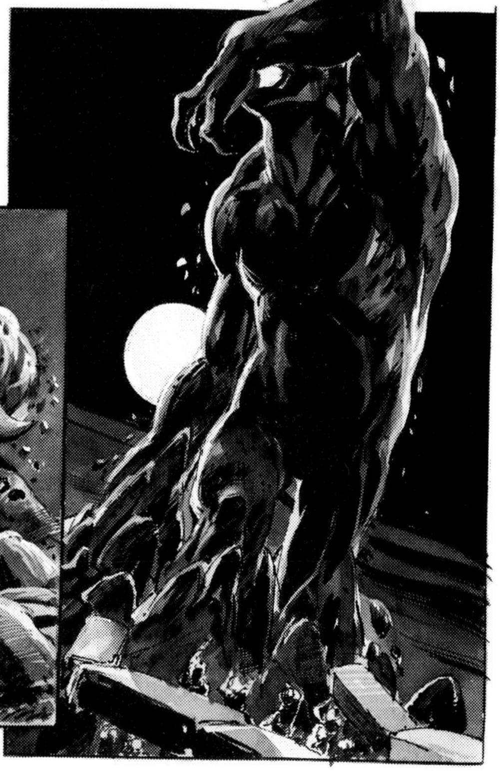

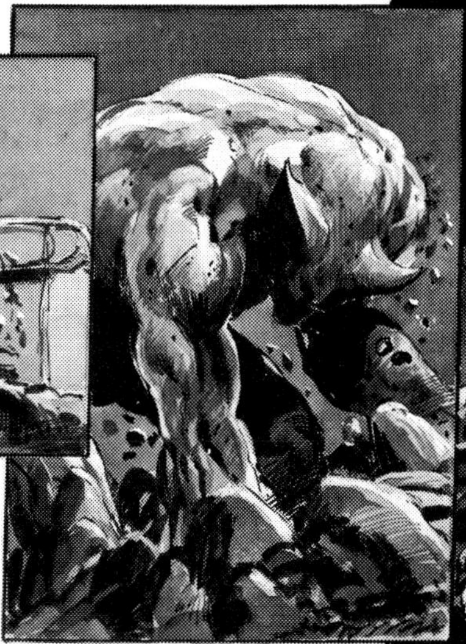

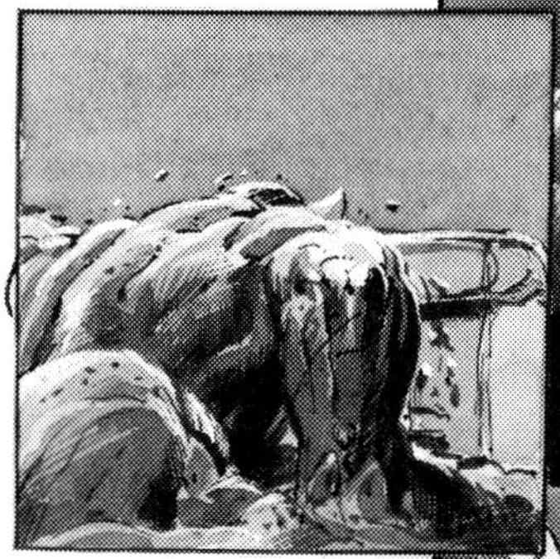

DIS, ROCK GOD, HAD COME AGAIN AS HE HAD COME ONE HUNDRED YEARS BEFORE, AND ONE HUNDRED YEARS BEFORE, AND ONE HUNDRED YEARS BEFORE THAT.

WORDS BROUGHT HIM. NEEDS BROUGHT HIM. FEAR OF ***NOT*** BRINGING HIM FORTH FROM HIS OWN BODY, THE EARTH, HAD BROUGHT HIM. NOT BECAUSE HE PROMISED LIFE AFTER DEATH, SALVATION, OR HARVESTS, AND PLENTIFUL RAIN. DIS WAS NOT A GOD OF PROMISE. HE WAS CALLED FORTH BECAUSE HE WOULD COME, CALLED OR NOT. BECAUSE HE WAS DIS, AND HIS BODY WAS THE VERY GROUND THEY WALKED. BECAUSE IT WAS NECESSARY FOR HIM TO STRIDE THE WORLD ONCE EVERY CENTURY. THERE WAS NO HUMAN EXPLANATION FOR HIS NEED... HE WAS DIS... IT WAS REASON ENOUGH.

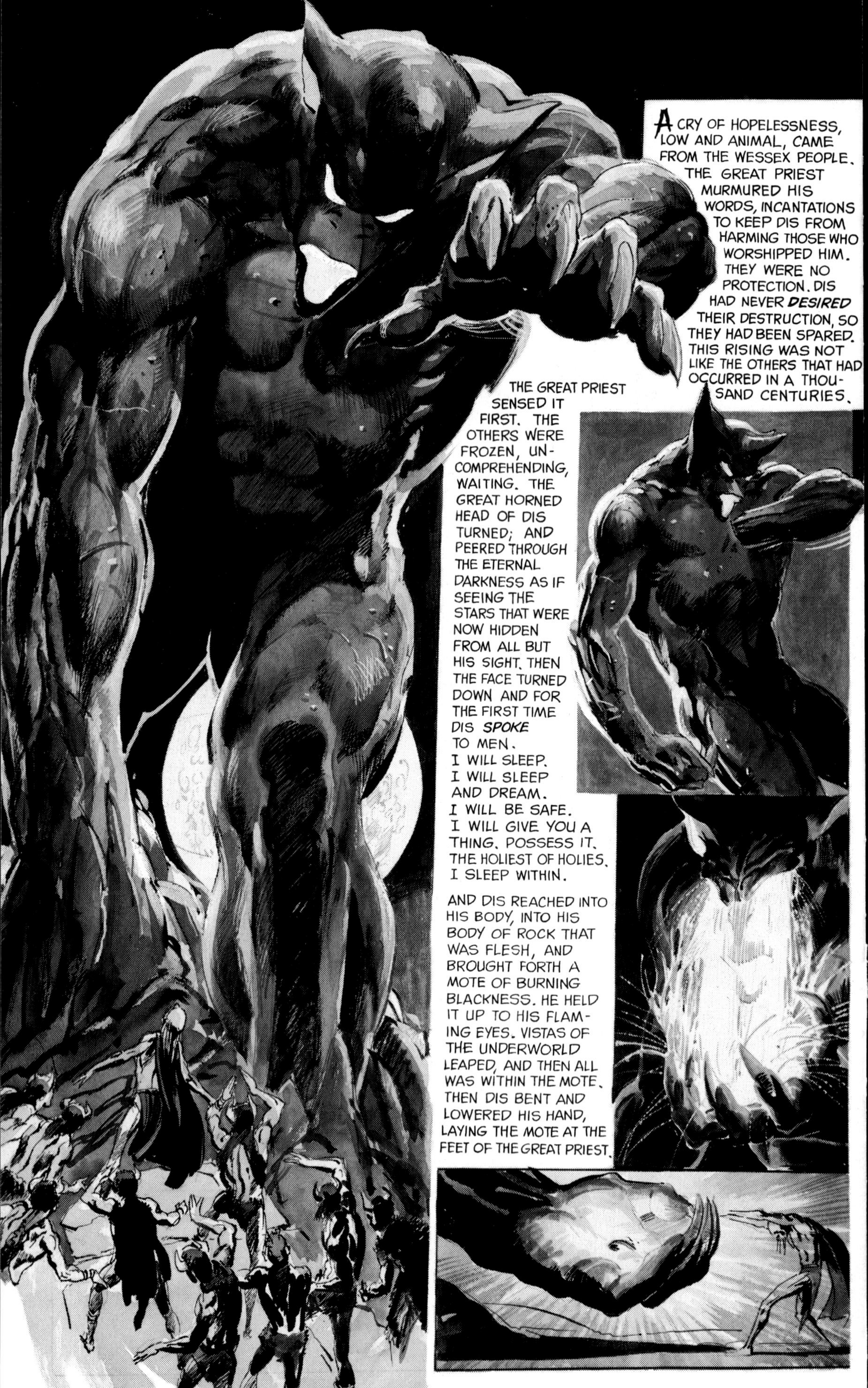
A CRY OF HOPELESSNESS, LOW AND ANIMAL, CAME FROM THE WESSEX PEOPLE. THE GREAT PRIEST MURMURED HIS WORDS, INCANTATIONS TO KEEP DIS FROM HARMING THOSE WHO WORSHIPPED HIM. THEY WERE NO PROTECTION. DIS HAD NEVER DESIRED THEIR DESTRUCTION, SO THEY HAD BEEN SPARED. THIS RISING WAS NOT LIKE THE OTHERS THAT HAD OCCURRED IN A THOUSAND CENTURIES.
THE GREAT PRIEST SENSED IT FIRST. THE OTHERS WERE FROZEN, UNCOMPREHENDING, WAITING. THE GREAT HORNED HEAD OF DIS TURNED; AND PEERED THROUGH THE ETERNAL DARKNESS AS IF SEEING THE STARS THAT WERE NOW HIDDEN FROM ALL BUT HIS SIGHT. THEN THE FACE TURNED DOWN AND FOR THE FIRST TIME DIS SPOKE TO MEN.
I WILL SLEEP.
I WILL SLEEP AND DREAM.
I WILL BE SAFE.
I WILL GIVE YOU A THING. POSSESS IT. THE HOLIEST OF HOLIES. I SLEEP WITHIN.
AND DIS REACHED INTO HIS BODY, INTO HIS BODY OF ROCK THAT WAS FLESH, AND BROUGHT FORTH A MOTE OF BURNING BLACKNESS. HE HELD IT UP TO HIS FLAMING EYES. VISTAS OF THE UNDERWORLD LEAPED, AND THEN ALL WAS WITHIN THE MOTE. THEN DIS BENT AND LOWERED HIS HAND, LAYING THE MOTE AT THE FEET OF THE GREAT PRIEST.

SUDDENLY THE YOUNG ACOLYTE PRIEST... WHO COULD NOT WAIT FOR SUCCESSION, WHO LUSTED AFTER POWER *NOW*... BROKE FROM THE MASS OF DARK, PRAYING SHAPES.

GREAT DIS!

NO!

THE GREAT PRIEST FEARED TO LOOK UP, BUT HIS WORDS WERE TO HIS GOD, TO ASSURE HIM THE LIFE OF ALL HIS PEOPLE WOULD BE SPENT PROTECTING THE HOLIEST OF HOLIES.

GREAT DIS, WE HAVE SERVED YOU FOR CENTURIES! NOW WE ASK A BOON.

I, MAG, DEMAND FOR YOUR FAITHFUL ONES WHO PLEDGE TO PROTECT YOUR SLEEPING SOUL THE BOON OF...

NONE EVER KNEW WHAT TOKEN THE ACOLYTE MIGHT HAVE DEMANDED TO RAISE HIMSELF TO A POSITION OF POWER. THE ROCK GOD REACHED DOWN AND DARKNESS FLOWED FROM HIS TALONED FINGERS. BLACK FIRE CONSUMED THE ACOLYTE IN AN INSTANT.

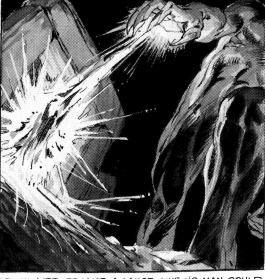

AND THE PILLAR OF BLACK FIRE SPARKLED UPWARD, THINNED, BECAME A LANCE-LINE NO MAN COULD LOOK INTO. THEN DIS HURLED THE BLACK FIRE INTO THE GROUND, WHERE IT BURNED THROUGH AND COULD BE SEEN TO SHIMMER. THE SOUND OF MAG'S SOUL SHRIVELING WAS A TREMBLING, TERRIBLE THING.

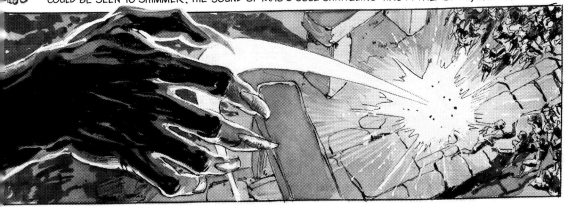

THEN DIS FLOWED BACK INTO THE EARTH, THE ROCKS BECAME ROCKS ONCE MORE, AND ALL THAT REMAINED WAS THE POWER STONE AT THE FEET OF THE GREAT PRIEST, WHO SHIVERED AND SPASMED FROM THE NEARNESS OF THE GOD'S VENGEANCE. THERE WAS A NEW ROCK IN STONEHENGE. IN ITS SURFACE WAS IMPRINTED THE MEMORY OF MAG. FOREVER HE WOULD LIVE IN PAIN, DEAD INSIDE THE ROCK, FOREVER BLACKLY BURNING IN AGONY. THEY TOOK THE MOTE AND KEPT IT HOLIEST OF HOLIES, AND DIS SLEPT.

DIS HAD SEPARATED HIMSELF SEVEN TIMES AND ONE MORE. TO LET HIS FLESH SLEEP WITH HIS SOUL WAS TO PERMIT THE CHANCE OF DESTRUCTION; HIS SOUL SLEPT WITHIN THE BLACK MOTE OF STONEHENGE. FROM SEVEN UNEARTHLY RISINGS HAD COME SEVEN STONES TO MATCH THE MOTE. THEY CAME TO BE KNOWN TO THE WORLD AS THE SEVEN STONES OF POWER FOR DIS KNEW A GOD EXISTS ONLY IF THERE ARE BELIEVERS; AND AS HE MUST SLEEP, FOR REASONS KNOWN ONLY TO GODS, HE MUST LEAVE BEHIND A LEGACY FOR LEGEND, BY WHICH HE WOULD BE REMEMBERED.

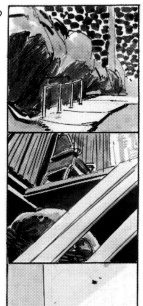

IN IRELAND, THE BLARNEY STONE.

THE STONE OF SCONE THAT CAME FROM SCOTLAND AND NOW LIVED BENEATH THE CORONATION CHAIR IN WESTMINSTER ABBEY.

THE GREAT RELIGIOUS SYMBOL OF ISLAM, THE BLACK STONE IN MECCA.

THE KOH-I-NOOR DIAMOND, WHICH THE PERSIANS CALLED THE MOUNTAIN OF LIGHT.

THE LOST STONE OF SOLOMON THAT HAD VANISHED FROM PALESTINE AND WHICH WAS SAID TO BE THE MOST TREASURED POSSESSION OF THE DALAI LAMA IN LHASA.

THE WELSHSTONE OF CHANGE 'PLINTH' THAT HAD LAST BEEN KNOWN TO RESIDE AT THE VACANT SEAT OF ARTHUR'S ROUND TABLE.

AND THE AMIDA OF DAIBUTSU, THE GREAT BUDDHA, IN THE SACRED TEMPLE OF KOBE IN JAPAN –THAT-WAS.

LEGEND AND THE WAYS OF MEN KEPT THESE POTENT STONES SECRETED. YET THERE WERE CHIPS, AND BITS, AND FROM *THEM* CAME THE GREAT SEAL OF SOLOMON, THE SILVER CRESCENT OF THE GREAT ANTHREX, THE TALISMAN OF SULEIMAN THE MAGNIFICENT, AND THE CIRCLE OF ISIS. BUT THEY COUNTED FOR LITTLE, DESPITE THEIR IMMENSE POWER.

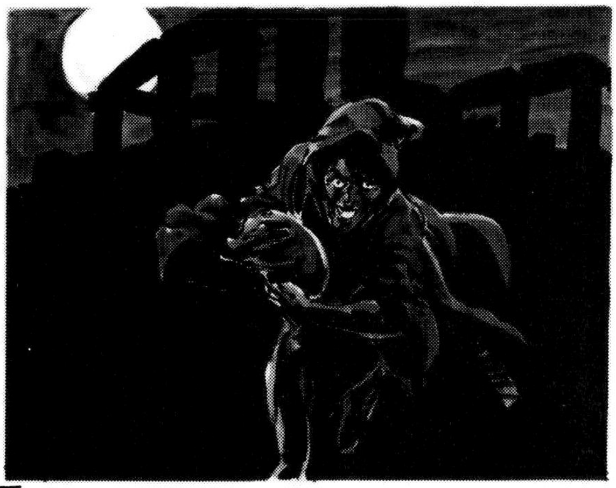

THIS IS WHAT HAPPENED TO THE BLACK SOUL MOTE. IT WAS DUG UP BY ONE WHO CAME IN THE NIGHT AND WAS MAD. AND SO, MAD, HE WAS NOT AFRAID.

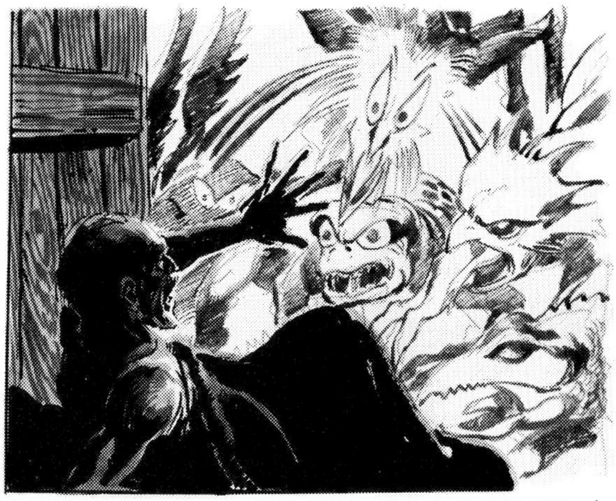

BUT HIS MADNESS DID NOT DETER THE TERRIBLE DEATH THAT CAME TO HIM, THE FLESH STRIPPED FROM HIS BODY AND EATEN BY THINGS ONLY PARTIALLY HIDDEN.

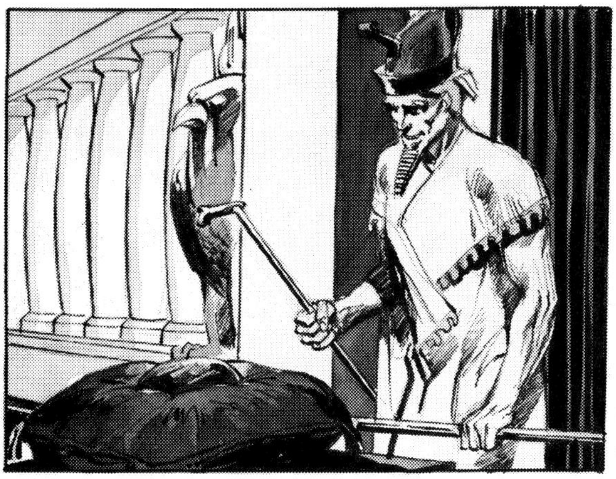

BUT HE HAD ALREADY TRADED THE MOTE TO ONE OF MINOAN CRETE. THAT ONE PASSED IT FOR GREAT WEALTH TO A THINKER OF MYCENAEAN GREECE OF WHOM IT WAS TAKEN IN RANSOM BY A PRIEST OF ISIS.

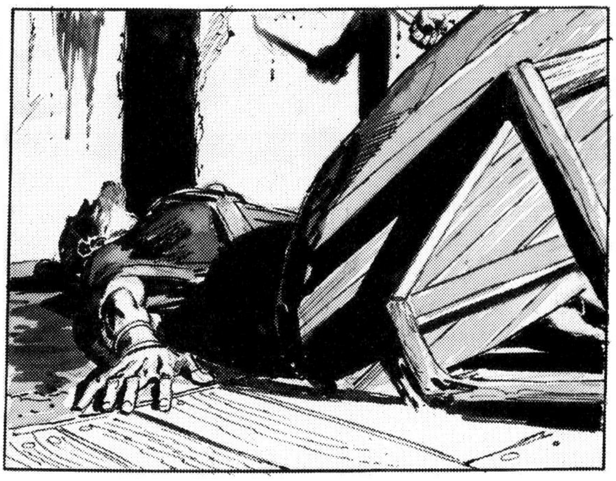

THE EGYPTIAN LOST IT TO A PHOENICIAN AND HE, IN TURN, LOST IT IN A GAME OF CHANCE THAT TOOK ALL HE OWNED, AS WELL AS HIS LIFE...

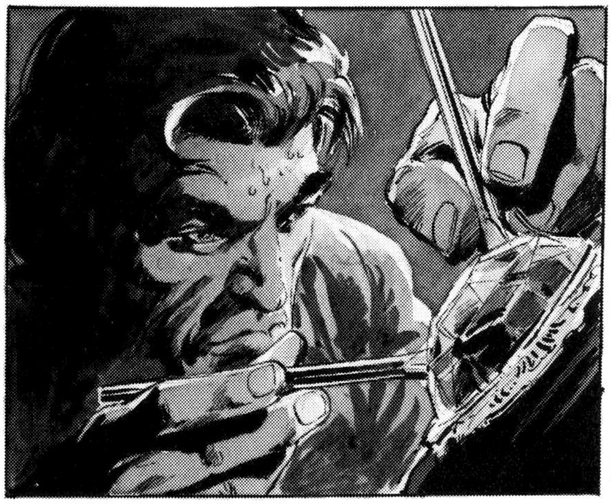

FROM HAND TO HAND IT TRAVELED, DOWN THROUGH THE CENTURIES, WITH DEATH AND SHAPES IN THE NIGHT FOLLOWING ITS JOURNEY. A THOUSAND HANDS, A THOUSAND MEN. TILL IT FOUND ITS WAY TO THE HAND OF AN ADVENTURER WHO ALSO WORKED IN SILVER.

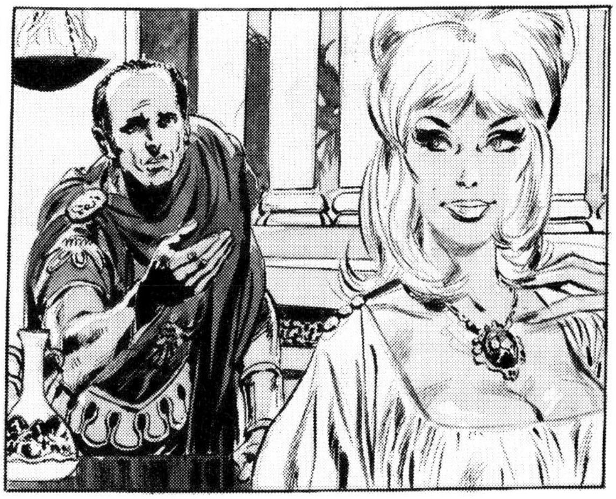

HE CLEANED IT AND POLISHED IT AND MOUNTED IT. THEN WOMEN OWNED IT. AND EACH WOMAN BECAME FAMOUS. THE NAMES ARE LEGEND. BUT ALWAYS THEY COVETED MORE, AND FINALLY REAPED THEIR REWARDS IN BLOOD.

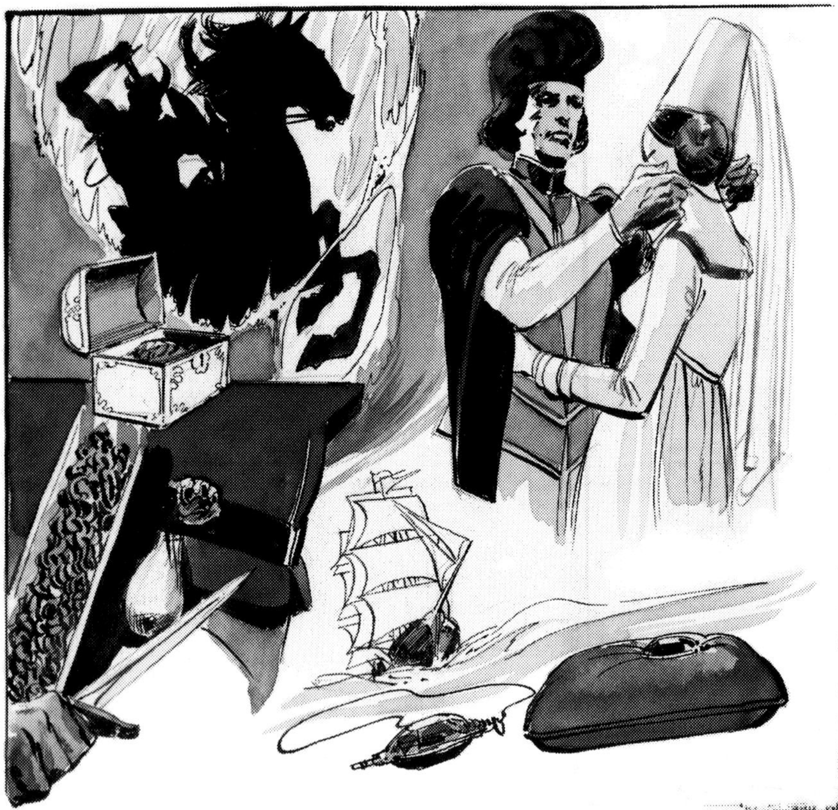

THE SOUL MOTE CAME ACROSS ANOTHER OCEAN, WHERE IT WENT FROM THE TREASURE HORDES OF OSMANSKI COSSACKS TO THE COFFERS OF POLISH NOBLEMEN, FROM THE DOWERIES OF PARISIAN ***DEMIMONDAINES*** TO THE CHAMOIS GOLD–SACKS OF ENGLISH VICARS, FROM THE POCKETS OF CUTPURSES TO THE NEW WORLD. AND THERE IT PASSES FROM BROOCH TO PENDANT, FROM RING TO LAVALIERE... AND WAS LOST.

...AND WAS FOUND:

BY A CROATIAN WORKMAN WHO HAD NO IDEA WHAT IT WAS, AND THREW IT WITH A SPADEFUL OF REFUSE, INTO THE HOLLOW CENTER OF THE CORNERSTONE OF A GREAT SKYSCRAPER.

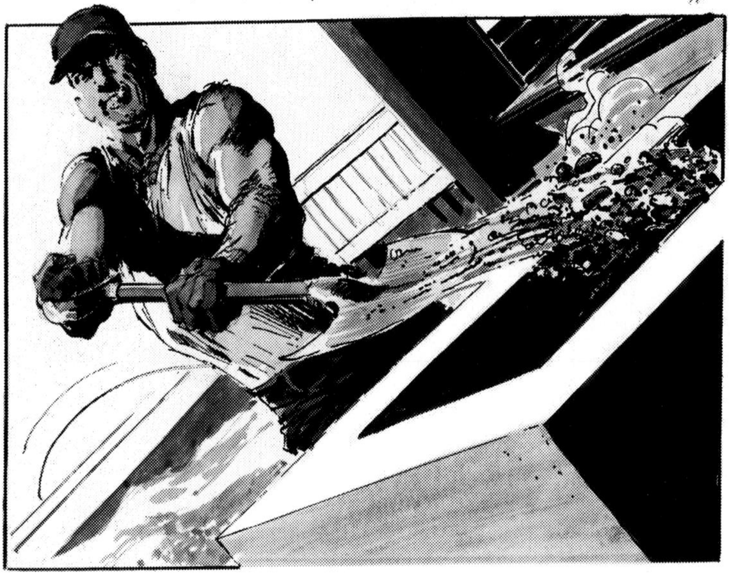

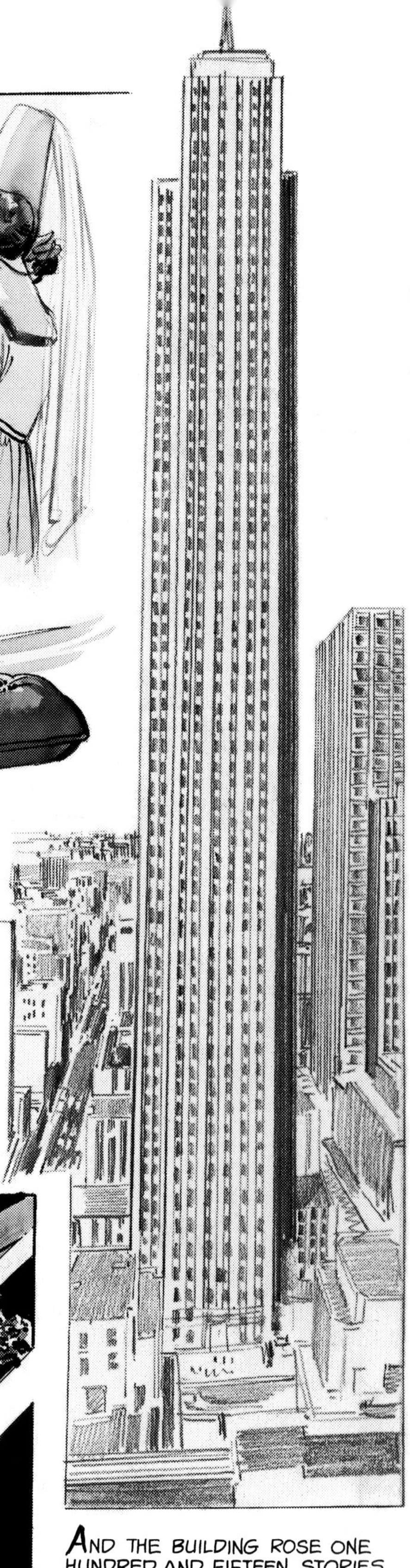

AND THE BUILDING ROSE ONE HUNDRED AND FIFTEEN STORIES OVER THE SLEEPING SOUL OF THE GREAT ROCK GOD DIS, WHO KNEW THE TIME WAS APPROACHING.

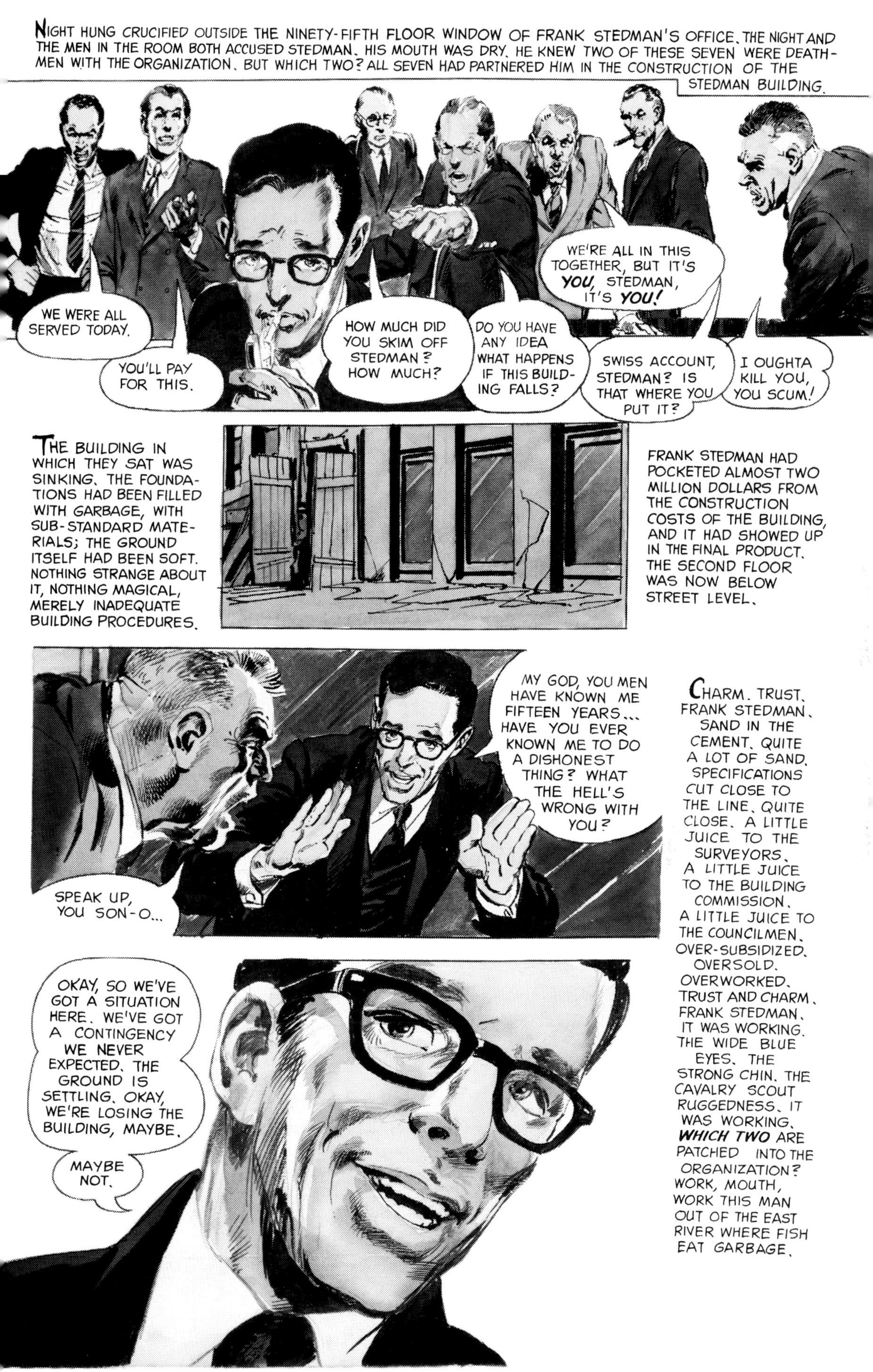
NIGHT HUNG CRUCIFIED OUTSIDE THE NINETY-FIFTH FLOOR WINDOW OF FRANK STEDMAN'S OFFICE. THE NIGHT AND THE MEN IN THE ROOM BOTH ACCUSED STEDMAN. HIS MOUTH WAS DRY. HE KNEW TWO OF THESE SEVEN WERE DEATH-MEN WITH THE ORGANIZATION. BUT WHICH TWO? ALL SEVEN HAD PARTNERED HIM IN THE CONSTRUCTION OF THE STEDMAN BUILDING.
WE WERE ALL SERVED TODAY.
YOU'LL PAY FOR THIS.
HOW MUCH DID YOU SKIM OFF STEDMAN? HOW MUCH?
DO YOU HAVE ANY IDEA WHAT HAPPENS IF THIS BUILDING FALLS?
WE'RE ALL IN THIS TOGETHER, BUT IT'S *YOU*, STEDMAN, IT'S *YOU!*
SWISS ACCOUNT, STEDMAN? IS THAT WHERE YOU PUT IT?
I OUGHTA KILL YOU, YOU SCUM!
THE BUILDING IN WHICH THEY SAT WAS SINKING. THE FOUNDATIONS HAD BEEN FILLED WITH GARBAGE, WITH SUB-STANDARD MATERIALS; THE GROUND ITSELF HAD BEEN SOFT. NOTHING STRANGE ABOUT IT, NOTHING MAGICAL, MERELY INADEQUATE BUILDING PROCEDURES.
FRANK STEDMAN HAD POCKETED ALMOST TWO MILLION DOLLARS FROM THE CONSTRUCTION COSTS OF THE BUILDING, AND IT HAD SHOWED UP IN THE FINAL PRODUCT. THE SECOND FLOOR WAS NOW BELOW STREET LEVEL.
SPEAK UP, YOU SON-O...
MY GOD, YOU MEN HAVE KNOWN ME FIFTEEN YEARS... HAVE YOU EVER KNOWN ME TO DO A DISHONEST THING? WHAT THE HELL'S WRONG WITH YOU?
CHARM. TRUST. FRANK STEDMAN. SAND IN THE CEMENT. QUITE A LOT OF SAND. SPECIFICATIONS CUT CLOSE TO THE LINE. QUITE CLOSE. A LITTLE JUICE TO THE SURVEYORS. A LITTLE JUICE TO THE BUILDING COMMISSION. A LITTLE JUICE TO THE COUNCILMEN. OVER-SUBSIDIZED. OVERSOLD. OVERWORKED. TRUST AND CHARM. FRANK STEDMAN. IT WAS WORKING. THE WIDE BLUE EYES. THE STRONG CHIN. THE CAVALRY SCOUT RUGGEDNESS. IT WAS WORKING. **WHICH TWO** ARE PATCHED INTO THE ORGANIZATION? WORK, MOUTH, WORK THIS MAN OUT OF THE EAST RIVER WHERE FISH EAT GARBAGE.
OKAY, SO WE'VE GOT A SITUATION HERE. WE'VE GOT A CONTINGENCY WE NEVER EXPECTED. THE GROUND IS SETTLING. OKAY, WE'RE LOSING THE BUILDING, MAYBE.
MAYBE NOT.

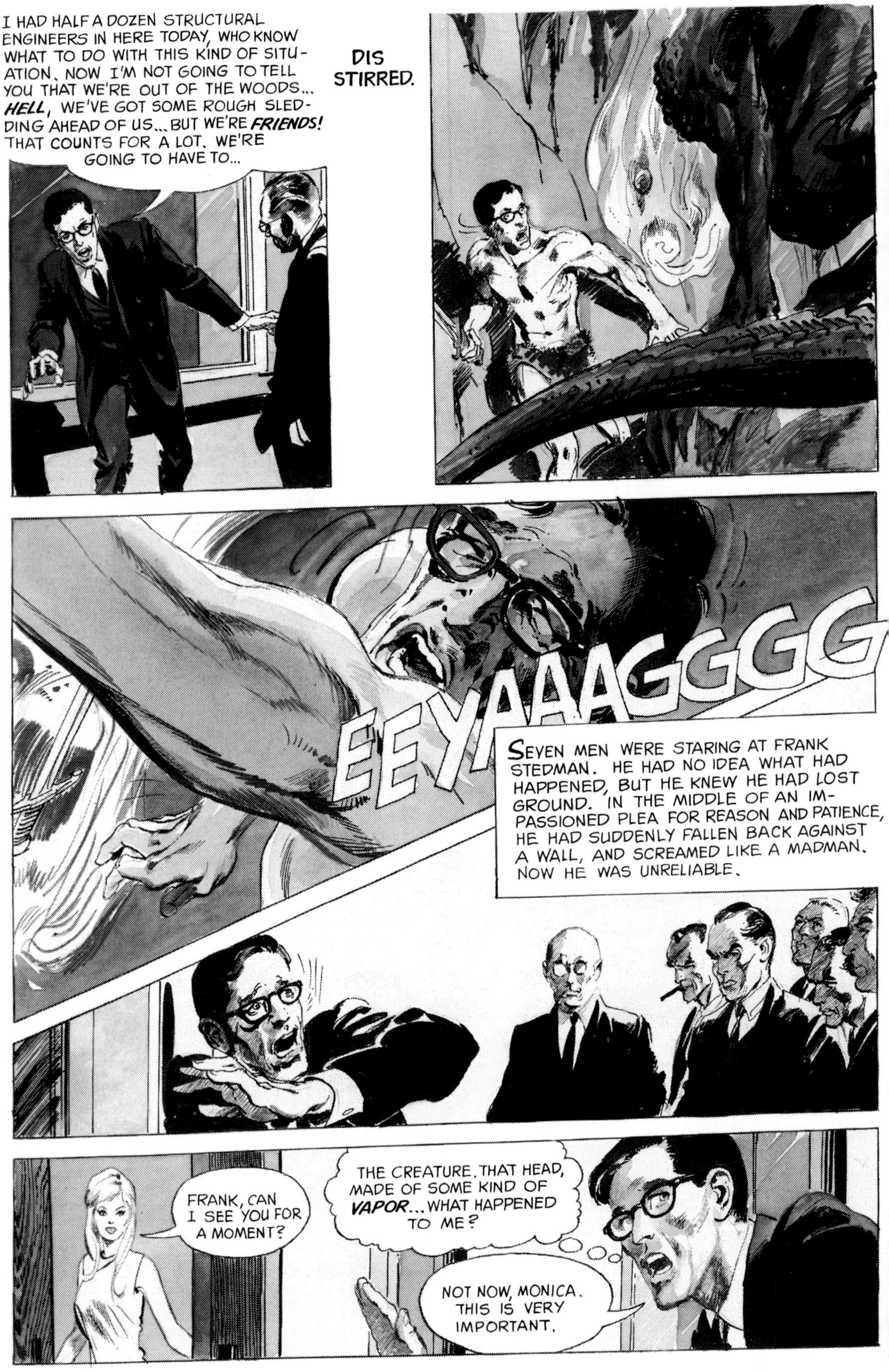

I HAD HALF A DOZEN STRUCTURAL ENGINEERS IN HERE TODAY, WHO KNOW WHAT TO DO WITH THIS KIND OF SITUATION. NOW I'M NOT GOING TO TELL YOU THAT WE'RE OUT OF THE WOODS... HELL, WE'VE GOT SOME ROUGH SLEDDING AHEAD OF US... BUT WE'RE FRIENDS! THAT COUNTS FOR A LOT. WE'RE GOING TO HAVE TO...
DIS STIRRED.
EEYAAAGGGGG
SEVEN MEN WERE STARING AT FRANK STEDMAN. HE HAD NO IDEA WHAT HAD HAPPENED, BUT HE KNEW HE HAD LOST GROUND. IN THE MIDDLE OF AN IMPASSIONED PLEA FOR REASON AND PATIENCE, HE HAD SUDDENLY FALLEN BACK AGAINST A WALL, AND SCREAMED LIKE A MADMAN. NOW HE WAS UNRELIABLE.
FRANK, CAN I SEE YOU FOR A MOMENT?
THE CREATURE. THAT HEAD, MADE OF SOME KIND OF VAPOR... WHAT HAPPENED TO ME?
NOT NOW, MONICA. THIS IS VERY IMPORTANT.

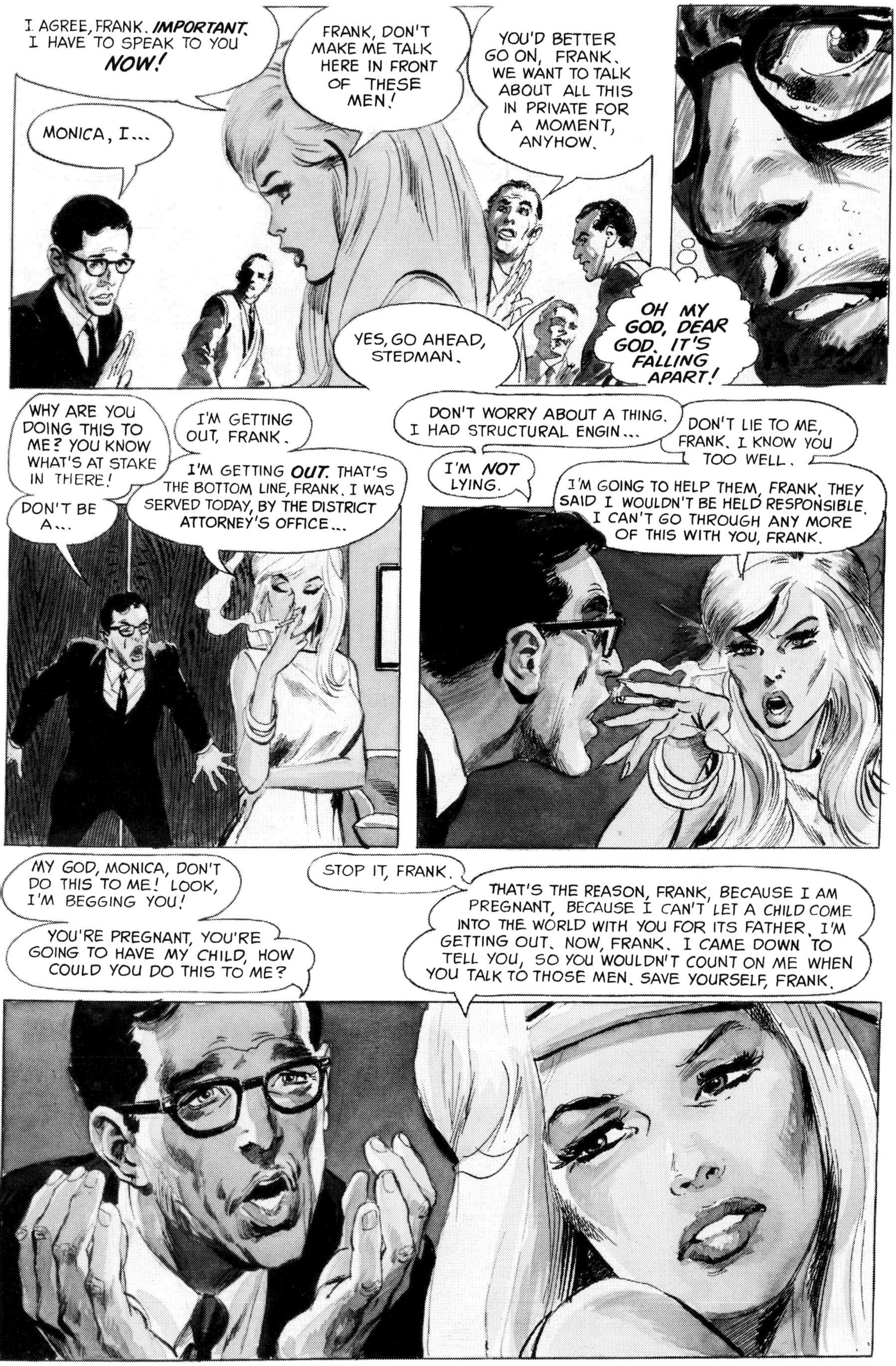

I AGREE, FRANK. IMPORTANT. I HAVE TO SPEAK TO YOU NOW!
FRANK, DON'T MAKE ME TALK HERE IN FRONT OF THESE MEN!
YOU'D BETTER GO ON, FRANK. WE WANT TO TALK ABOUT ALL THIS IN PRIVATE FOR A MOMENT, ANYHOW.
MONICA, I...
YES, GO AHEAD, STEDMAN.
OH MY GOD, DEAR GOD. IT'S FALLING APART!
WHY ARE YOU DOING THIS TO ME? YOU KNOW WHAT'S AT STAKE IN THERE!
DON'T BE A...
I'M GETTING OUT, FRANK.
I'M GETTING OUT. THAT'S THE BOTTOM LINE, FRANK. I WAS SERVED TODAY, BY THE DISTRICT ATTORNEY'S OFFICE...
DON'T WORRY ABOUT A THING. I HAD STRUCTURAL ENGIN...
DON'T LIE TO ME, FRANK. I KNOW YOU TOO WELL.
I'M NOT LYING.
I'M GOING TO HELP THEM, FRANK. THEY SAID I WOULDN'T BE HELD RESPONSIBLE. I CAN'T GO THROUGH ANY MORE OF THIS WITH YOU, FRANK.
MY GOD, MONICA, DON'T DO THIS TO ME! LOOK, I'M BEGGING YOU!
YOU'RE PREGNANT, YOU'RE GOING TO HAVE MY CHILD, HOW COULD YOU DO THIS TO ME?
STOP IT, FRANK.
THAT'S THE REASON, FRANK, BECAUSE I AM PREGNANT, BECAUSE I CAN'T LET A CHILD COME INTO THE WORLD WITH YOU FOR ITS FATHER. I'M GETTING OUT. NOW, FRANK. I CAME DOWN TO TELL YOU, SO YOU WOULDN'T COUNT ON ME WHEN YOU TALK TO THOSE MEN. SAVE YOURSELF, FRANK.

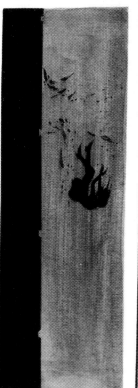

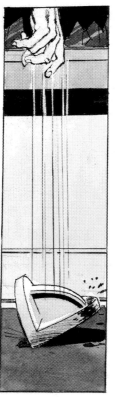

STEDMAN TWITCHED WITH COLD, A SUDDEN COLD THAT CAME FROM A PLACE HE COULD NOT NAME. *AH WEGH THOGHA*. HE WANTED TO SCREAM, BUT THE TREMBLING WAS ON HIM, HIS BODY WAS HELPLESS IN THE SPASTIC GRIP OF THE SEIZURE.

THOSE WORDS, WHAT WERE THOSE WORDS?...

AH WEGH THOGHA!

HIS THROAT HAD NEVER BEEN TAUGHT TO FORM THOSE WORDS, BUT IT DID.

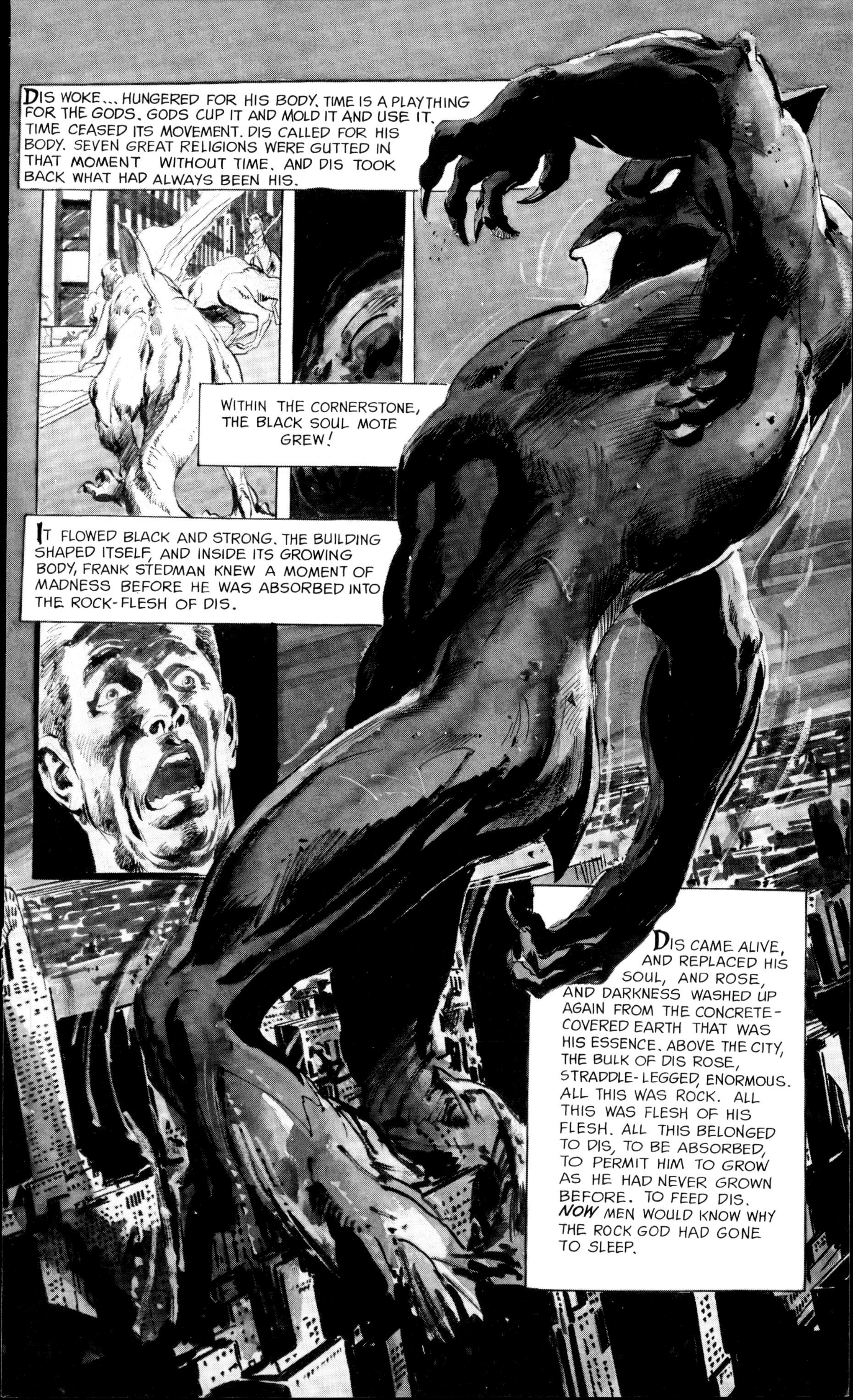
DIS WOKE... HUNGERED FOR HIS BODY. TIME IS A PLAYTHING FOR THE GODS. GODS CUP IT AND MOLD IT AND USE IT. TIME CEASED ITS MOVEMENT. DIS CALLED FOR HIS BODY. SEVEN GREAT RELIGIONS WERE GUTTED IN THAT MOMENT WITHOUT TIME, AND DIS TOOK BACK WHAT HAD ALWAYS BEEN HIS.
WITHIN THE CORNERSTONE, THE BLACK SOUL MOTE GREW!
IT FLOWED BLACK AND STRONG. THE BUILDING SHAPED ITSELF, AND INSIDE ITS GROWING BODY, FRANK STEDMAN KNEW A MOMENT OF MADNESS BEFORE HE WAS ABSORBED INTO THE ROCK-FLESH OF DIS.
DIS CAME ALIVE, AND REPLACED HIS SOUL, AND ROSE, AND DARKNESS WASHED UP AGAIN FROM THE CONCRETE-COVERED EARTH THAT WAS HIS ESSENCE. ABOVE THE CITY, THE BULK OF DIS ROSE, STRADDLE-LEGGED, ENORMOUS. ALL THIS WAS ROCK. ALL THIS WAS FLESH OF HIS FLESH. ALL THIS BELONGED TO DIS, TO BE ABSORBED, TO PERMIT HIM TO GROW AS HE HAD NEVER GROWN BEFORE. TO FEED DIS. NOW MEN WOULD KNOW WHY THE ROCK GOD HAD GONE TO SLEEP.

Word by word, he'll take you over the edge.

Volume 1 contains *Over the Edge* and *An Edge in My Voice*.
ISBN 1-56504-960-8
$21.99 US/ $29.99 CAN
Available now.

Volume 2 contains *Spider Kiss* and *Stalking the Nightmare*.
ISBN 1-56504-961-6
$21.99 USA/$29.99 CAN
Available November 1996.

Volume 3 available in May 1997.

Harlan Ellison unleashes controlled chaos with 31 razor-sharp EDGEWORKS. Each book of the 20-volume collection contains completely revised, updated and expanded text as well as an original introduction by the multiple award-winning author who has **thrilled, provoked, angered, perplexed, amazed,** and **delighted** his audience for over 40 years.

"... a masterful storyteller whose goal is to leave you with a bittersweet taste-like a jalapeño-laced cinnamon bear."
-Playboy

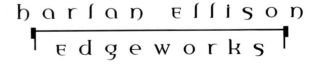

**Available at your favorite bookseller.
Call 1-800-454-WOLF
for information.**